# MARCO

# COPENHAGEN

D0633017

**with** local tips •

The author's special recommendations are
highlighted in yellow throughout this guide

*There are five symbols to help you find your way around this guide:*

★

*Marco Polo's top recommendations – the best in each category*

◈

*sites with a scenic view*

◉

*places where the local people meet*

♟

*places where young people get together*

**(96/A1)**
*pages and coordinates for the Street Atlas of Copenhagen*
**(U/A1)** *coordinates for the General Map inside front cover*
*For your orientation even places that are not marked in the
Street Atlas are provided with coordinates.*

*This travel guide was written by Sabine Neumann and
Horst Schwartz. They own an editorial office, which specializes
in tourism. They travel often to Denmark.*

# MARCO ⊕ POLO

*Travel guides and language guides in this series:*

Alaska • Algarve • Amsterdam • Australia/Sydney • Bahamas • Barbados
Barcelona • Berlin • Brittany • Brussels • California • Canada • Channel Islands
Chicago and the Great Lakes • Copenhagen • Costa Brava/Barcelona
Costa del Sol/Granada • Crete • Cuba • Cyprus • Dominican Republic
Eastern Canada • Eastern USA • Egypt • Florence • Florida • French Riviera
Gran Canaria • Greek Islands/Aegean • Hong Kong • Ibiza/Formentera
Ireland • Israel • Istanbul • Italian Riviera • Jamaica • Lanzarote • London
Los Angeles • Madeira • Mallorca • Malta • Menorca • Mexico • Netherlands
New York • New Zealand • Normandy • Norway • Paris • Portugal • Prague
Rhodes • Rocky Mountains • Rome • San Francisco • Scotland • South
Africa • Southwestern USA • Switzerland • Tenerife • Thailand • Turkish
Coast • Tuscany • USA: New England • USA: Southern States • Venice
Washington D.C. • Western Canada • Western USA

French • German • Italian • Spanish

*Marco Polo would be very interested to hear your
comments and suggestions. Please write to:*

*North America:*
*Marco Polo North America*
*70 Bloor Street East*
*Oshawa, Ontario, Canada*
*(B) 905-436-2525*

*United Kingdom:*
*GeoCenter International Ltd*
*The Viables Centre*
*Harrow Way*
*Basingstoke, Hants RG22 4BJ*

*Cover photograph: Anzenberger: Bastin & Evrard*
*Photos: Fotex: Naumann (9), New Pix (21); O. Heinze (60); Kluyver (30); Mauritius: Ley (95);
Vidler (11); M. Pasdzior (4, 12, 16, 29, 34, 44, 50, 54, 66, 70, 76, 79, 86); P. Santor (24);
B. Skyum (6, 33, 41, 65, 72); A. Sperber (56, 81); Transglobe: Svensson (46)*

*1ˢᵗ edition 2001*
*© Mairs Geographischer Verlag, Ostfildern, Germany*
*Translator: Jane Riester*
*English edition 2001: Gaia Text, Munich*
*Editorial director: Ferdinand Ranft*
*Chief editor: Marion Zorn*
*Cartography for the Street Atlas: © Hallwag AG, Bern*
*Design and layout: Thienhaus/Wippermann*
*Printed in Germany*

# CONTENTS

# Discover Copenhagen!

*Copenhageners are friendly and broad-minded.*
*Observations from the Danish capital and*
*compliments for the Queen*

Copenhagen is Copenhagen. In contrast to other major cities, no one would dream of comparing the "merchant harbour" (København means just that) with other cities in an attempt to describe its beauty. Copenhagen is Copenhagen, and that's that. And for many, it is still the most beautiful city in Europe.

Admittedly this can only be said of the inner city, which is small, compact and cosy, *hyggelig,* as the Danes would say. Old Copenhagen is bordered to the north-west by an almost semi-circular ring of lakes, Skt. Jørgens Sø, Peblinge Sø and Sortedams Sø. To the north stands the Citadel, to the east the harbour and in the south is the Town Hall Square. Within this sector, the old town centre is an incomparably beautiful, intact collection of buildings, roads, squares, fountains and passageways. The houses are generally well cared for and the older ones have been carefully

*The city's pulsating lifeline:*
*the Strøget*

restored. The roads in the old town are paved with cobblestones. At the Nyhavn, time seemingly stands still: historic wooden ships bob up and down in front of the candy-coloured backdrop of well-preserved town houses from the 17th and 18th centuries which stand along the harbour front. The branch canal transports the nautical atmosphere right into the heart of the city.

Copenhagen escaped the bombing of World War II. It was in 1807, though, that the old town suffered a similar bombardment at the hands of the British naval fleet, which reduced numerous houses to rubble. At this time, however, there was not much left of the old Copenhagen, whose reputation as the most beautiful European capital was known throughout the world. Devastating fires had already destroyed large areas of the royal seat which had been established here in the 17th century. The "old" Copenhagen we see today is the result of the reconstruction work which followed the fires and the attack by the British, with the exception of a few Renais-

*Splendour of a past age: the crown jewels in the Rosenborg Palace*

sance structures which managed to survive all these disasters. The majority of these buildings were commissioned by Christian IV, who reigned from 1588 to 1648, and include the old Stock Exchange, the Rosenborg Palace and the Round Tower. Also apparently untouched by the passing centuries is the Christianshavn district (named after its founder) on the other side of the harbour branch, which is in many ways reminiscent of Amsterdam.

Copenhagen lies on the east coast of the island of Zealand (Sjælland), the largest of the Danish Baltic Sea islands. From the city, the Copenhageners look out across the Sound (Øresund), the busy strait separating Zealand and the coast of southern Sweden. Scarcely had the Danes begun building the gigantic bridge link across the Great Belt – which now joins Jutland and Fyn in the west with Zealand and the capital – than they began work on a second, no less fascinating bridge project. Now, Copenhagen and the town of Malmö in southern Sweden are linked by a four-lane highway and a double-track railway running above and (partly)

below the Øresund, creating a joint economic and residential zone. Just how expensive and complicated it was to design the ideal bridge construction to suit the natural surroundings is vividly illustrated in an impressive exhibition in the Øresund Udstilling information centre at the marina in Kastrup. This new fixed link has not only brought closer the southern Swedish province of Skåne – which has always felt more akin to its Danish neighbour than to its monarchy in far-off Stockholm – but also the whole of Sweden and Norway seem a step nearer to Copenhagen and therefore the rest of Europe. Travelling times from north to south have been drastically cut as a result.

At the moment, the Øresund region is on everyone's lips in Copenhagen. Every two years, a three-month Øresund Festival is held, called *kulturbro,* the "Bridge of Culture". The majority of the seven hundred cultural institutions in the new region will take part. Experts estimate that even more people will move out of Copenhagen in future to live in the countryside, which will increasingly mean in Sweden. People travelling from the Malmö area to Copenhagen now take less than one hour for the journey.

The city's population has been on the decline for some years now. In 1950 there were 770,000 inhabitants in Copenhagen itself, now there are scarcely 500,000. On top of this are the 85,000 who live in Frederiksberg, a self-governing commune right in the heart of Copenhagen. What the Danes call *Storkøbenhavn*, i.e. the conurbation of Copenhagen, includes, in addition to the city proper, all its suburbs which are independent communities and go to make up the administrative region of *Københavns Amt* with some 630,000 inhabitants. When outsiders speak of "Greater Copenhagen", however, they mean the *Hovedstadsregion*, that is the capital and the fifty surrounding communities in which a total of 1.75 million people live. To put this in perspective, Denmark as a whole has a population of 5.2 million.

Originally, Copenhagen was just a small fishing village called, quite simply, "Havn". In 1158, as a reward for his feudal loyalty in the battle for the Danish crown, the victorious Waldemar the Great gave the village to his comrade-in-arms Absalon (1128–1201). The deed of gift unfortunately no longer exists. At the same time, he conferred upon Absalon – a descendent of the noble Hvide line and former student of theology in Paris – the title of Bishop of Roskilde. Later, in 1177, he became Archbishop of Lund. The pugnacious Absalon, who was seemingly as much a man of the sword as of the cloth, had a castle built in 1167 to defend his property on the site of today's Christiansborg. Copenhagen was born. The ruins of Absalon's medieval castle can still be viewed today underneath Christiansborg Palace. By the time Christoffer III (of Bavaria) made Copenhagen his royal seat in 1443, the town had some 10,000 inhabitants. Christian I, who was later to found the university, was the first king to be crowned in Copenhagen. A coronation ceremony as such has not been performed for a Danish monarch since democracy was introduced in 1849 during the Three Years' War (1848–1850). The king's crown was packed off to the treasure chamber at the Rosenborg Palace and has never bedecked a royal head since, not even on the most important occasions. On the death of the monarch, though, the crown, along with the sabre and all ceremonial medals, is laid on top of the coffin. This was last the case when Frederik IX died in 1972.

He was succeeded by his eldest daughter Margrethe Alexandrine Thorhildur Ingrid, who was born on 16 April 1940, just a few days into the German occupation of the country. She ascended the throne as Margrethe II, but only in a figurative sense, since both thrones in the throne room at the Christiansborg Palace are no longer used! Nowadays, when the Queen holds a reception, she stands at the far end of the room, and once the audience is over, the guests may quite happily turn their backs on her and make for the door.

The Queen is very popular in her country. "In Denmark, even the opponents of the monarchy are fans of the Queen," say the Danes, jokingly. The oldest monarchy in the world shows not the slightest sign of wear, due certainly to a large extent to the fact that the Queen performs her duties with the utmost prudence. Visitors to Copenhagen may even witness the sight of a Rolls-Royce bearing the royal standard waiting patiently at a red traffic light on Kongens Nytorv, while the pedestrians cross the square. Like any good citizen, the Queen abides by the traffic regulations. Margrethe II, who studied philosophy, constitutional law and archaeology, has a gift for all things artistic. She enjoys painting and drawing and, some years ago, designed two hundred costumes and the set for a production of the ballet *Et Folkesagn* at the Royal Theatre.

Conscripts in Denmark consider it an honour and a privilege when they are commanded to serve in the Queen's Life Guards during the final two months of their nine-month national service. The fact that, during their two-hour guard duty in the courtyard of the Amalienborg Palace, they occasionally wink at the odd tourist or whisper from between apparently closed lips the answer to a curious visitor's question is a sign of the casual attitude so typical of the Danes, even on such a dignified occasion. As it is, they have their own particular, straightforward relationship towards the armed forces – as they do towards their national flag. The "Dannebrog" (which simply means flag of the Danes or red cloth) as it is called, is, incidentally, the oldest in the world.

A further reason for the Danes' respect for their royal family is surely the uncompromising attitude shown by King Christian X

during the occupation of the country by German troops in April 1940. Matters came to a head between the two sides in August 1943, when the Danish government refused to declare a state of emergency on their own part, as had been demanded by the occupying forces. This led to the dismissal of the government, the dissolution of parliament and the disarmament of the army. The King himself was placed under house arrest at the Amalienborg Palace. The events of these years are documented in an impressive display at the Frihedsmuseet, which is devoted to the story of the Danish resistance from 1940–1945.

Freedom is for the people of Copenhagen, as for all Danes, their most treasured possession, though they also value and respect the right of others to their own opinions and lifestyle. The prime example of their tolerance is the story of the "Fristaden Christiania", the Free City of Christiania, which began with an illegal land occupation in 1971. At that time, the armed forces had just abandoned roughly 30 ha of land, complete with barracks, huts and ramparts, in the district of Christianshavn on the Amager peninsula. The military site was to be cleared to make way for a residential area, but before the plans could be put into practice, a group of young people took over the site and the buildings on it. In the autumn of 1971 the drop-outs and alternative thinkers, the homeless and the hippies declared the foundation of the Fristaden Christiania, in a quest for a truly democratic form of society. During the first few years, the squatters faced vehement opposition and condemnation from conservative local politicians, whereas the majority of the population was not unsympathetic towards this "social experiment", as the politicians called it. The political discussion which ensued provoked many a harsh word – quite out of character for the otherwise so amiable Danes. Eviction orders were issued and attempts were made to clear the site, culminating in what can only be described as a battle between the police and the residents of Christiania. In the meantime, however, the inhabitants of the free city have managed to rid themselves of all excesses of drug-taking, violence and crime, and the autonomous Christiania community is no longer merely tolerated. To mark the twentieth anniversary of its founding, the Danish state finally gave its official blessing, as it were, and contractual agreements were drawn up with the authorities which regulate mutual rights and obligations of the two sides. Since then, one side pays its taxes and, in return, the other side has laid on electricity and water supplies. Right from the start, the profits which the 800 to 1,000 inhabitants have made from, for example, running bars and staging cultural events, have flowed back into their own social and cultural projects, thereby saving the state a considerable sum of money. Visitors to Copenhagen who are keen to come and see this alternative-style district – some 50,000 per year, it is estimated – are advised to show a little tact and respect towards their hosts and not pester them for snapshots. The last thing the "Free City" wants to become is just another tourist attraction!

The best and quickest way for you the visitor to get to know the people of Copenhagen is to take a walk down the legendary Strøget, a chain of roads, actually, and the city's first and longest pedestrian zone. For many guests, it is also its greatest attraction. The "Strip" is not just a shopping street, but also the ideal place to see and be seen, a meeting point for all manner of peo-

*The "Free City" of Christiania: living proof of Danish tolerance*

ple, whether on their own or in a group, in the first flush of youth or with a lifetime of experience behind them. Anyone who gets married in Copenhagen spends at least part of their last night of freedom here, the groom with his "stags" and the bride with her "hens" – sometimes even in daring costumes. In a nutshell, Strøget is simply irresistible. If you have a little time on your hands, it's easy to gain a first impression of the people in the capital, by stopping off at one of the cafés – at the first hint of fine weather, the tables appear outside – and watching the world go by. The Copenhageners are not quite as relaxed as you may have imagined; they're just as rushed off their feet as the citizens of any other major city. But despite all that, they remain polite, cheerful even. It's hard not to, amidst the sound of the many street musicians who often enough transform the Strøget into one giant open-air concert.

A bench in the Tivoli is also a good observation point, if you want to learn more about the locals. The Tivoli is not merely an amusement park and it is certainly nothing like your common or garden funfair. It is an institution, without which the city wouldn't be the same, say the Copenhageners. In 1842 a journalist called Georg Carstensen was granted permission by King Christian III to create an amusement park on a site which had formed part of the ring of fortifications surrounding the entire town centre. His colleagues even recorded how many hands he had to shake – 3,615 – when he welcomed each visitor in person on the day his park opened on 15 August 1843! At least once a year, every self-respecting Copenhagener pays a visit to Tivoli, some even dressing up for the occasion. Families in particular, often several generations together, enjoy going for an afternoon stroll here, and as the day draws to a close and the coloured lights come on, each family member eagerly awaits the famous Tivoli firework display, the spectacular culmination of every visit – if the kids can stay up that late!

One thing which strikes the visitor to Tivoli is the way children are treated here. They are not excessively "mothered", it seems, and teenagers enjoy more freedom than their foreign counterparts. The Danes – and the people of Copenhagen are no exception – are very fond of children. Not that they put on an exaggerated show of it. Instead, it's the little things which convince you of their sincerity. Play areas, for example, are a matter of course in shops, banks, museums and other public buildings. It is therefore easier for visitors to contemplate bringing their children with them to Copenhagen for a holiday than to many other cities. However, those who scold their whining children when the walk around town becomes tiring or boring – not to mention those who hit their children in public – meet with harsh criticism from passers-by. Even Danish tolerance has its limits.

The weeks leading up to Christmas are a very special time in Copenhagen. The atmosphere in the festively decorated city casts an irresistible spell on every visitor, and the obvious, child-like anticipation of the festivities to come is infectious. This is also the time when the special Christmas

*Life for the Copenhageners wouldn't be the same without Tivoli*

postage stamps, the colourful *julemærker* are sold. The postage-paid stamps are designed by notable artists and the proceeds go towards financing children's homes.

As a visitor, you'll find it easy to get chatting to the locals, in cafés, bars or museum restaurants, for example. The people here have a weakness for all things satirical and they love making ironic remarks, even in a foreign language; English is almost second nature to them.

*Tak*, thank you, and *mange tak*, thank you very much, are the words you will probably hear the most during your stay in Copenhagen. The locals watch their p's and q's very carefully, and that means saying thank you at every possible opportunity. They say thank you for an invitation, thank you when they arrive and thank you when they leave again. They even like to phone up later and say thank you for the wonderful evening they've just had. Should the host and guest bump into each other at a later date, it is never a mistake to say thank you one more time! So don't forget: have your *tak* and *mange tak* at the ready at all times! Don't worry, though: no Copenhagener will take offence if one of their foreign guests forgets the occasional *tak* now and then. After all, the Danes are extremely tolerant, aren't they?

# Exploring the city

*The compact old town invites you to take a dose of culture. Have a break for a picnic in the park. There's a royal palace around (nearly) every corner*

Of all the European capitals, Copenhagen is the one which makes life easiest for the visitor. Nine out of ten of the not-to-be-missed attractions lie within the small, approximately 4 sq km old town centre. The key points of reference are the Citadel in the north, the Tivoli amusement park in the south, the Botanical Garden in the west and the harbour and Nyhavn (new harbour) in the east. This is precisely the area which was at one time completely enclosed by a massive defensive ring, built to protect Copenhagen against enemy attack. These fortifications have long since given way to parks and other open spaces, and the Danish capital now welcomes foreign "intruders" with open arms. Car drivers can quite happily leave their vehicles at home, for two reasons. Firstly, the municipal authorities actively discourage car driving by radically limiting the amount of parking space available. Secondly, the inner city can easily be explored on foot, provided you remember to wear sensible shoes to negotiate the cobblestones successfully! When your feet are crying out for a rest, help is at hand in the form of numerous cafés, outdoor restaurants, benches and idyllic corners to take a break in. Take up the invitation and enjoy a rest on your sightseeing tour – take a leaf out of the Danes' book and give yourself time to relax. The few major sights which lie outside the city centre can be reached easily and cheaply (with the Copenhagen Card, free of charge) using public transport, and when you consider the short distances involved, even a taxi ride wouldn't cost the earth.

It is impossible to "do" the whole of Copenhagen in one visit, unless of course you have a whole week at your disposal. Generally, that means you'll have to come again to discover the attractions which lie outside the immediate city centre. A visit to the district of Christianshavn is a must for the "advanced" visitor, as is a trip to the Frederiksberg commune or a stroll through the Vesterbro and Østerbro quarters,

*The Stock Exchange with its unusual dragon's tail tower dates back to the time of Christian IV.*

13

which give you a good introduction to "young" Copenhagen.

## BREWERY

**Carlsberg** (103/D6)
J. C. Jacobsen named his brewery in the suburb of Valby after his small son Carl and the world-famous beer was brewed here for the first time on 10 November 1847. His son Carl went on to extend the Ny-Carlsberg brewery complex. The guided tour through the beer-drinker's mecca – whose symbol is its Elephant Tower carried by four elephants made of Bornholm granite – no longer takes you through the actual production plant, but to the new visitor centre. This includes the original, museum-like brewery premises from 1847, the stables and exhibition rooms documenting the history of the brewery. At the end of the tour, there's a chance to sample the goods!

You bump into the Jacobsens, figuratively speaking, all over Copenhagen, in their role as patrons of cultural projects. The Ny Carlsberg Glyptotek owes the backbone of its collection to them, and the Ny Carlsberg Fund contributes on a large scale to the cultural life of the city. Here, beer drinking and the arts go hand in hand, say the Copenhageners with a wry smile. *Mon–Fri 10 am–4 pm;*

---

# MARCO POLO SELECTION: SIGHTSEEING

**1 Bakken**
Tivoli's older and more traditional competitor (page 15)

**2 Frederiksberg Have**
The park in which the Copenhageners celebrate weddings and other special occasions (page 32)

**3 Tivoli**
More than just an amusement park: heaven on earth for 30,000 visitors per day (page 16)

**4 Christians Kirke**
The church which looks like a theatre inside (page 20)

**5 Grundtvigs Kirke**
Cathedral made of six million bricks (page 20)

**6 Gråbrødretorv**
Possibly the most beautiful square in the city and definitely one of the liveliest (page 25)

**7 Rosenborg Castle**
The Renaissance palace and one-time court junk room (page 28)

**8 Nyhavn**
The road along the harbour has smartened up its reputation – in the true sense of the word (page 30)

**9 Strøget**
More than just a shopping street, the "Strip" is the lifeline of the city (page 31)

**10 Christianshavn**
A touch of Amsterdam in Christian IV's quarter (page 31)

*admission: free; Gamle Carlsberg Vej 11, Valby; www.carlsberg.com; S: Valby; bus: 6, 10, 18*

### GARDENS, PARKS, AMUSEMENT PARKS

**Danmarks Akvarium** (U/E4)

The aquarium is one of the largest and most attractive in Europe. At weekends (and during Danish school holidays) you can even touch some of the fish! There are numerous, fascinating tanks, simulating various types of seascape and living conditions, from permanent darkness to artificial breakers. *Jan–mid-Feb, end of Oct–Dec: Mon–Fri, 10 am–4 pm, Sat–Sun, 10 am–5 pm; mid-Feb–end of Oct: daily 10 am–6 pm; admission: adults: 60, children: 30 dkr; Kavalergården 1, Charlottenlund; www.danmarksakvarium.dk; S: Charlottenlund; regional train: Hellerup; bus: 6, 166, 169, 176, 179*

**Assistens Kirkegård** (103/E1)

This "auxilliary cemetery" was established in 1757, in the wake of the experiences of 1711 when the plague claimed so many victims that the existing burial grounds proved insufficient. This is Copenhagen's most beautiful cemetery and has become a popular place for picnicking and sunbathing. Many famous people are buried here, including Hans Christian Andersen (Section P), the philosopher Søren Kierkegaard (Section A) and the writer Martin Andersen Nexø (*Pelle the Conquerer*, near the entrance). *Nørrebrogade; bus 5, 16, 350 S*

**Bakken** (U/E4)

★ ✿ ☂ This amusement park which lies to the north of the city is the oldest in Denmark; older than the Tivoli Gardens and much more traditional in style. Fewer tourists find their way to these pleasure grounds which were established around four hundred years ago.

Bakken lies on the edge of the *Dyrehaven*, a wooded park with plenty of game. *End of Mar.–end of Aug. midday–midnight; admission: free; Dyrehavsbakken Klampenborg; www.bakken.dk; S and regional train: Klampenborg; bus: 6, 185, 388*

**Library Garden** (97/D6)

After that tiring sightseeing tour, put your feet up in the garden of the Royal Library in the company of the philosopher Søren Kierkegaard (1813–1855). The library is over three hundred years old, though it has only been housed in the current building since 1906. The small park is a peaceful oasis in the middle of town. *Børsgade; daily 9 am–7 pm; bus: 1, 2, 6, 8, 10, 37, 550 S, 650 S*

**Botanisk Have** (96/B-C1-2)

The ten-hectare Botanical Garden was created in 1874. The large Palm House, built in the same year and renovated in 1982, takes pride of place. In comparison to other, similarly attractive botanical gardens, the Botanisk Have distinguishes itself mainly by its collection of every native plant of Denmark, Iceland, the Faeroe Islands and Greenland. *Palm House: daily 10 am–3 pm; greenhouses: Wed, Sat and Sun, 1 pm–3 pm; garden: daily 8.30 am–6 pm (in winter until 4 pm only); admission: free; Gothersgade 128/Øster Farimagsgade 2c; www.botanicgarden.ku.dk; S and regional train: Nørreport; bus: 5, 10, 14, 16, 31, 40, 42, 43, 184, 185, 350 S*

*The 1874 Palm House takes pride of place at the Botanical Garden*

### Tivoli Gardens (96/A–B6)

★ ☼ Twenty-five nostalgic carousels turn in the Tivoli Gardens alongside ultra-modern rides, all embedded in a sea of 400,000 flowers. Twenty-eight eating houses, ranging from garden cafés to top-class restaurants, offer 10,000 seats and cater for an average of 30,000 visitors per day. One of these can be found in a reconstruction of a 19th-century frigate, moored on the banks of the Tivoli lake.

The oldest of the numerous historic buildings on the site is the pantomime theatre in the Chinese Pavillion, dating back to the year 1874. Every evening, except Sundays, Pierrot, Harlequin and Colombine tread the boards here, keeping alive the tradition of the *Commedia dell'Arte*, the Italian Renaissance comedy form. The crowds at each performance are so large, that enterprising individuals rent out ingenious mirror constructions to enable spectators to see the stage over the heads of those in front!

Despite the busy funfair atmosphere, the park becomes truly idyllic in the evening, illuminated by some 110,000 lights (glaring neon lights are frowned upon, though). This is when Tivoli's theatres and concert halls really come into their own. Around 150 concerts are staged here each year, in which world-famous solo artists and orchestras often take part, a fact which underlines the vital contribution which Tivoli makes to the cultural life of Copenhagen. Many a Danish musician has begun his career in the band of the Tivoli Boys Guard, which was founded in 1844, one year after the opening of the amusement park. The Guard consists of 110 boys between the ages of nine and sixteen, who march through the park at 8.30 pm on Saturdays and Sundays. Three times a week, on Wednesday, Friday and Saturday, a firework display is put on at 11.45 pm. In the weeks leading up to Christmas, the park – otherwise closed in winter – is transformed into a huge Christmas market. *Mid-April–mid-Sept.: Sun –Thurs, 11 am–midnight, Fri–Sat, 11 am–1 am; mid-Nov.–Christmas: Christmas market, Sun–Thurs, 11 am–9 pm, Fri–Sat, 11 am–10 pm; admission: adults: 39–45, children: 25–30 dkr; Vesterbrogade 3; www.tivoli.dk; S and regional train: København H.; bus: 1, 2, 6, 8, 10–14, 16, 28–30, 34, 40, 67–69, 150 S, 250 S, 550 S, 650 S*

## Zoo (102/B4–5)

Copenhagen's zoo enjoys a good reputation world-wide, due to the many rare species among the 2,000 animals which are kept here. The Tropical House is particularly worthy of praise. Beware: if you're visiting the zoo with children, you are unlikely to get much further than the children's zoo, with its collection of touchable and strokeable little inmates! *Nov.–Mar.: daily 9 am–4 pm; April–May: Mon–Fri, 9 am–5 pm, Sat–Sun, 9 am–6 pm; June–Aug.: daily 9 am–6 pm; Sept.–Oct.: daily 9 am–5 pm; admission: adults: 70, children: 35 dkr; Roskildevej 32; www.zoo.dk; bus: 6, 18, 28, 39, 100 S, 550 S, 832*

## BUILDINGS

### Old Stock Exchange (97/D5)

With its tower resembling four interwoven dragon's tails, the old Stock Exchange on the Slotsholmen Island is one of the most striking and well-known buildings in the city. Christian IV had it built between 1619–1625. Today, this Renaissance structure, which is reminiscent of a storehouse – and

served as one at one point – is the home of the Chamber of Commerce. *Børsgade; bus: 1, 2, 6, 8, 10, 37, 550 S, 650 S*

### Citadel (97/F1)

Once a year, on the Citadel's "birthday", the windmill turns again – windmill? Yes, it was built in 1687, and stands, looking rather out of place now, in this pentagonal fortress which was begun in 1662 by Frederik III. There used to be a bakery here too, to bake bread for the soldiers. The barracks, which are still used today by military units and the home guard, date back to the beginning of the 18th century, as does the less austere, two-storey Commandant's house and the church. Directly next to the church is the guardroom, from where prisoners could participate in religious services without leaving the prison. The tiny museum dedicated to the Royal Rifle Corps (closed in winter) provides a welcome change on a walk around the barracks and big guns, defences and ditches of the Citadel. Bordering on the site is the Churchill Park, in which stands the Anglican St. Alban's Church (1885–1887). It was built in the English (neo-) Gothic style and has recently been renovated. The mighty *Gefion Fountain* next to the church symbolises the origin of the island of Zealand. Created by Anders Bundgaard in 1908, it depicts the goddess Gefion, who, at the bidding of Odin, travelled to Sweden to obtain more land. She transformed her four children, sons of a giant, into oxen and in the space of one night ploughed up an area the size of Zealand. Sweden's King Gylfe presented her with this land as a gift and her sons pulled it out into the Baltic Sea: Zealand was born. *Daily 6 am until sunset; Churchill Park/Langelinie; bus: 1, 6, 9*

## Town Hall (96/B5–6)

☙ The gold-plated statue of the city's founder Absalon (1128–1201) adorns the façade of the Town Hall, which was officially opened in 1905. Absalon is depicted in his bishop's vestments. The figure is the work of sculptor Christian Gottlieb Vilhelm Bissen, who was also responsible for the equestrian statue on Højbro Square (1901). The latter shows not Absalon the bishop (and later archbishop), but rather Absalon in his capacity as a military commander astride his rearing horse. The plinth underneath the monument was designed by Martin Nyrop, architect of the Town Hall, details of which were clearly inspired by the Italian Renaissance. The multi-storey Great Hall is particularly impressive – perhaps glass-roofed inner courtyard is a better description. It serves as a venue for exhibitions and other festivities. The greatest attraction at the Town Hall is the World Clock, constructed by the inventor Jens Olsen (1872–1945). It took him 27 years to make and was not put in position until in 1955. The clock has twelve separate mechanisms and shows, among other things, local time, solar time, sunrise and sunset, the Gregorian Calendar and the constellations in the sky. The Town Hall tower is almost 106 m high, the highest in the country, and once you've scaled the three hundred or so steps, you'll be rewarded with a truly unforgettable view. The Town Hall Square has the highest volume of traffic in the city and, in the evening, is illuminated by the biggest and brightest neon signs.

Also on the front of the Town Hall is a relief set above a doorway, showing a bunch of grapes. This was intended as the entrance to a public house in the cellar. The plan was never realised, since the then strictly teetotal city council vetoed it!

The *Dragon Fountain* with its unusually shaped basin was erected on the Town Hall Square in 1904. Incredibly, there was something missing in the original design, namely the bull against which the dragon was supposed to be fighting. The bronze sculpture was added some 19 years later by Joakim Skovgaade.

A further decorative addition to the square is the *Statue* of the writer Hans Christian Andersen, at the junction with the boulevard which bears his name. There is also a representation of two *lur players* in bronze, set on a tall column. A lur is a sacred instrument from the Bronze Age. Around 35 lures have been discovered in peat bogs in Denmark, some of which can be seen in the National Museum. It is even possible to coax a few notes out of them – they sound rather like the modern trumpet. The modern, flat-roofed structure, built in 1996 when Copenhagen was the European City of Culture, and which closes the north-western side of the square, is still a thorn in the flesh of many Copenhageners. Critics would like to see the 36-million-Krone eyesore pulled down, or at least reduced in size. Originally it was a centre for information on annual culture events, now it offers advice on matters of city administration and local public transport. *Town Hall open to visitors: Mon–Fri, 10 am–3 pm; admission: free; guided tours: Mon–Fri, 3 pm, Sat, 10 am; admission: adults and children: 30 dkr; tour of the tower: June–Sept.: Mon–Fri, 10 am, midday, 2 pm, Sat, midday; Oct.–May: Mon–Sat, midday; admission: adults and children: 20 dkr; World Clock: Mon–Fri, 10 am–4 pm, Sat 10 am–1 pm; admission: adults: 10, children: 5 dkr; Rådhuspladsen; www. copenhagencity.dk; S and regional train: København H.; bus: 1, 2, 6, 8, 14, 16, 19, 27–30, 32, 33, 46, 64, 68*

## Round Tower (104/C3)

🔆 Czar Peter the Great, on his visit to Copenhagen, is said to have ascended the Round Tower *(Rundetårn)* in a four-horse carriage. The idea is not quite as ridiculous as it may seem. Joined to the Holy Trinity Church at one end, this huge structure was built as an observatory and completed in 1642 under Christian IV. In its heart, it features a 209-m-long and very wide spiral corridor. The observation platform, which can be reached via a narrow spiral staircase, is located at the top of the 36 m high tower and affords the most beautiful view across the city. From here in the observatory, it is possible to do a little star-gazing!

The Round Tower was originally intended as the bell tower of the *Holy Trinity Church,* which truly lives up to its name. It was consecrated in 1656, having taken 19 years to build, and served as the University Church, the University Library and – thanks to the tower – as an observatory. Incidentally, the bells were never housed in the Round Tower! The library, including some extremely valuable manuscripts, was situated directly under the church roof and was almost completely destroyed in the fire which raged through the city in 1728. Today, the church, tower, old university buildings and student residences present a harmonious picture. In fine weather, the streets round about are filled with young people.

The best view of the Round Tower can be had from the Regensen student hall of residence (entrance in Store Kannikestræde). *Tower: June–Aug.: Mon–Sat, 10 am–8 pm, Sun, midday–8 pm; otherwise Mon–Sat, 10 am–5 pm, Sun, midday–5 pm; Oct.–Mar., also Tues–Wed, 7 pm–10 pm (the observatory is only open at this time); admission: adults: 15, children: 5 dkr; Købmagergade 52 A; www.rundetaarn.dk; S and regional train: Nørreport; bus: 5, 14, 16, 31, 42, 43, 73 E, 173 E, 184, 185, 350 S*

## The Black Diamond (97/D6)

The ultra-modern extension to the Royal Library is linked to the old building by a bridge and owes its name to the material used to build it, namely African black granite. The building houses not only valuable collections belonging to the library including manuscripts, musical scores and drawings, but is also home to the National Photographic Museum and serves as an exhibition and concert hall. *Christians Brygge 9; www.kb.dk; exhibitions: Mon–Sat, 10 am–7 pm; admission: free; tour of the building: admission: 20 dkr; bus: 5, 11–13, 30, 34, 40, 47, 250 S, 543 P (Langebro) or 2, 8, 9, 28, 31, 37, 72 E, 73 E, 79 E, 350 S (Børse)*

## Tycho Brahe Planetarium (103/F4)

The planetarium is the largest in Europe and was named after the astronomer Tycho Brahe (1546–1601). He was held to be the most important astronomer prior to the invention of the telescope, and discovered a new star (Nova Cassiopeia) in the Cassiopeia constellation. The exhibitions are of an extremely high educational standard and cover not only astronomy, but also space travel. The space theatre boasts a projection surface of 1,000 sq m. The building, designed by Knud Munk and opened in 1989, is a stunning example of contemporary architecture, its façade reflected in the Skt. Jørgens Sø. This lake, together with the Peblinge Sø and the Sortedams Sø, forms a semi-circular ring around old Copenhagen. The terrace of the planetarium restaurant also opens onto the lake and, logically enough, is called "Cassiopeia". *Tues–Thurs, 9.45 am–9 pm, Fri–Mon, 10.30 am–9 pm; admission: adults: 15 dkr, children: 5 dkr; Gammel Kongevej 10; www.tycho.dk; S: Vesterport; regional train: København H.; bus: 1, 14, 16*

## CHURCHES

### Christians Kirke (105/D4)
★ You can't help being reminded of the theatre when you enter Christan's Church in Christianshavn. The church was consecrated in 1759, and the walls are lined with galleries, which extend over three floors, and are reminiscent of theatre boxes. Another astounding detail is the arrangement of the altar, pulpit and organ, one above the other, in the centre of one long side of the building. The crypt is accessible from the outside and runs the full length of the church. It is divided into 48 burial chapels which are mostly separated by wrought-iron grillwork. There are also a number of graves underneath the floor, dating back

to the 1960s. *Daily 8 am–6 pm; (Nov.–Feb., only until 5 pm); Strandgade; bus: 2, 8, 9, 31, 37*

### Grundtvigs Kirke (U/E5)
★ For 19 years, between 1921 and 1940, one master bricklayer and six journeymen laid six million yellow bricks to complete the church which was dedicated to Bishop Nikolaj Frederik Severin Grundtvig, a very popular man in Denmark, even today. Grundtvig (1783–1872) was a parish priest before becoming Bishop of Zealand. He was a historian, translator of Nordic sagas and a poet. He also composed 271 of the 754 hymns in the Danish hymn book. His major claim to fame, however, is as founder of the Folk High Schools in Denmark, which enjoy considerably higher status than comparable institutions abroad.

The architect of this mighty building, which holds 1,800 worshippers, never lived to see it completed; Peder Vilhelm Jensen Klint, born in 1853, died in 1930. The urn containing his ashes is set into the wall of the church vestibule. Kare Klint, his son and also an architect (and acclaimed furniture designer) completed the church according to his father's plans. Klint senior was also responsible for the development of the area around the church.

The western façade together with the tower remind the onlooker of an organ. The church as a whole is a synthesis of typical Danish village church and Gothic cathedral. The three-nave interior is 35 m wide, 22 m high and 76 m long, and is astonishingly light. It is the work of Kare Klint and his son Esbe. They deliberately left the brick walls bare, to best set off their

*You bump into Hans Christian Andersen rather a lot in Copenhagen*

colour and texture. *End of Mar.–Oct.: Mon–Sat, 9 am–4.45 pm, Sun, midday–4 pm; Nov.–end of Mar.: Mon–Sat, 9 am–4 pm, Sun, midday– 1 pm (except during services); På Bjerget (Bispebjerg district); S: Emdrup; bus: 10, 16, 19, 43, 69*

## Helligånds Kirke (96/C4)

Right in the middle of the bustling city, on the Amagertorv, the Church of the Holy Ghost stands in an idyllic spot in a small yard surrounded by wrought-iron railings. It is often the venue for exhibitions and concerts and consequently plays a more active role in the lives of the Copenhageners than many of the city's other churches.

The predecessor of today's brick church was probably built at the beginning of the 14th century, extended in the middle of the 15th century, and ceded to the monastery which was founded here in 1474. It was badly damaged in the fire of 1728 and subsequently reconstructed. The sandstone portal, from the year 1620, was actually designed for incorporation in the old Stock Exchange. *Mon–Fri, midday–4 pm, Sun, 10 am–midday; service with music: Mon–Fri, midday; Amagertorv; bus: 27–29, 42, 43*

## Holmens Kirke (97/D5)

A church with a colourful history. The original, much smaller building, dating back to 1562, was used as an anchor smithy. In 1619, it was converted into a naval church. Today, it serves as one of the Royal Family's places of worship. It was here, in the Renaissance structure, that the wedding of Queen Margrethe II and her French husband, Prince Henrik, took place. *Mid-May–mid-Sept.: Mon–Fri, 9 am– 2 pm, Sat, 9 am–midday; mid-Sept.–mid-May: Mon–Sat, 9 am– midday; Holmens Kanal; bus: 1, 2, 6, 8–10, 31, 37, 43*

## Marmorkirke (97/E2)

The Norwegian marble from which it is made gave this church its popular name (its proper title, Frederiks Kirke, is never used). Despite its huge dimensions – the dome is 46 m high and has a diameter of 31 m – this is not Copenhagen's cathedral, but an ordinary parish church. Star architect Nicolai Eigtved also drew up the plans for the entire Frederiksstaden district, including the four buildings which constitute the Amalienborg Palace. If he had had his way, the church would have turned out even bigger; it was, after all, intended to commemorate the Royal Family's 300th anniversary. The foundation stone was laid in 1749, and the excavated hole was 30 m deep. It was no wonder that the Crown eventually ran out of money for the project. Eigtved died in 1754 and consequently did not experience the shame of seeing building work halted in 1770. The ruins were a tourist attraction in themselves for over a hundred years, until an industrialist called C. F. Tietgen bought the entire site and paid for the completion of the church – on a smaller scale. *Mon, Tues, Thurs–Sat, 10.30 am– 4 pm, Wed, 10.30 am–6 pm, Sun, midday–4.30 pm; guided tours (for details, call Tel. 33 15 01 44; don't forget to state which language!): June–Aug.: daily; Sept.–May: Sat–Sun only, 1 pm and 3 pm; access to dome: admission: adults: 20, children: 10 dkr; mid-June–Nov.: Mon–Fri, 1 pm and 3 pm; Dec.–mid-June: Sat–Sun, 1 pm and 3 pm; Frederiksgade; bus: 1, 6, 9*

## Nikolaj Kirke (97/D4)

You wouldn't think so, looking at it from the outside, but the Nicolaj Church is a reconstruction of a much older building. The ruined tower of the 13th-century church was all that remained in the wake of the great fire of 1795 which devastated Copenhagen. The site was gradually taken over by market-stall holders, who eventually had to make way for the new church in 1917. The tower was rebuilt in 1910. Today, the church contains a café-restaurant and is a centre for contemporary art, playing host to changing exhibitions and concerts. *Daily, midday–5 pm; admission: adults: 20 dkr, children: free; Nikolaj Plads; Tel. 33 93 16 26; bus: 1, 2, 6, 8, 10, 43*

## Petri Kirke (96/B4)

The history of St. Peter's Church has been ridden with disaster. The previous building, first mentioned in 1304, and probably the oldest church in the city, burnt down in an earlier city fire in 1386. The interior of the structure which replaced it in 1450 fell victim to the conflagration of 1728. Finally, in 1807, the bombardment of Copenhagen by the British fleet almost sealed the church's fate. Fortunately, the expert renovation work has healed the old wounds. The Gothic nave and chancel are particularly fascinating, as is the ring of burial chapels dating back to the 17th century. In the 15th century the church was misused as a foundry for bells and cannons, before being passed over to the German community in Copenhagen in 1585, to whom it has belonged ever since. *Sat only, 1 pm–3 pm; admission: adults: 20, children: 10 dkr; Nørregade/Skt. Peders Stræde; bus: 5*

## Vor Frelsers Kirke (97/F6)

The spiral staircase which takes you up the spire of Our Saviour's Church runs partly inside and partly outside the tower! At the top of the tower, built between 1749 and 1752, is a statue of Christ set on a golden sphere. It is well worth scaling the four hundred steps to the top of the 99-m-high spire to enjoy the breathtaking view over Christianshavn and the whole of Copenhagen. When you get your breath back, don't forget to take a look at the precious Baroque interior of the church itself, which is older than the tower (built between 1682 and 1696) and includes the altar (1732), the font and the pulpit (1773) and the organ (1698). *A charming carillon chimes every hour; a longer piece, the "Hymn of the Season" is played at 9 am, midday, 3 pm, 6 pm, 9 pm and at midnight. Carillon concerts: Sat, 5 pm, Sun, midday. Church and tower (the latter may be closed, depending on the weather):*

*April–Aug.: daily 11 am–4.30 pm; Sept.–Oct.: daily 11 am–3.30 pm; Nov.–Mar.: (church only) 11 am–3.30 pm. Admission: adults: 20, children: 10 dkr; Prinzessegade/Skt. Annae Gade; bus: 2, 8, 9, 31, 37, 350 S*

## Vor Frue Kirke (96/B4)

Copenhagen's cathedral, Our Lady's Church, appears remarkably modest from the outside. The classical building was constructed in 1811–1829 as a replacement for the Baroque cathedral which was destroyed by British cannons in 1807. The Baroque structure was the sixth church to stand on this site, all of which were destroyed by fire, the last in 1728. Sculptor Bertel Thorvaldsen created not only the John the Baptist frieze for the tympanum on the western façade, reminiscent of a Greek temple, but also the figures of Christ and the Apostles in the interior and the figure of the kneeling angel supporting the font. *Mon–Thurs and Sat, 9 am–5 pm, Fri, 9 am–10.30 am and midday–5 pm, Sun, midday–4.30 pm; Oct.–April: Sun, midday–1.30 pm and 3 pm–4.30 pm; Nørregade, Frue Plads; entrance: Dyrkøb; S and regional train: Nørreport; bus: 5*

## SQUARES

## Amagertorv (96/C4)

🕏 The city fathers had no money to spare, so it was left to the proprietors of the luxury shops on the Amagertorv to finance the redesigning of the square by an art professor, using expensive, many-coloured flagstones. Both the street and the square known as Amagertorv, around the *Stork Fountain* (erected in 1894) form the busiest and noblest section of the lively shopping and pedestrian zone, Strøget. Until 1864, this was the site of the fruit and vegetable market, selling produce from the island of Amager, which is linked to Copenhagen by a bridge and is now the home of the city's airport. It is hard to imagine that the fountain was once a popular meeting place for hippies and later the rallying point for the restless '68 generation. In those days, barefoot guitar players and even, in fine weather, nude bathers were a common sight. It is still a magnet for the young today, although their presence is no longer seen as provocative by residents and visitors. The more polished image of the square is due in part to the underground public toilets (2 dkr), which are luxurious to say the least. No less opulent are the shops on the Amager Square, which are without exception all located in historic houses, the most beautiful being No. 6, which was built in 1660 in the Dutch Renaissance style. *S: Nørreport; bus: 27–29, 42, 43*

## Axeltorv (96/A5–6)

🕏 It is only comparatively recently that the Axeltorv became a pedestrian zone. Despite several attempts to enhance its appearance with, for example, a pond and several sculptures, it still cannot be considered one of the more attractive of the city's squares. The candy-coloured *Palads,* both a cinema and multi-purpose venue, stands here, built in 1914 to stage the performances of the circus dynasty Benneweis. The entertainment centre *Scala* fulfils a similar purpose, housing a few shops, several cinemas, cafés and restaurants, which unfortunately are beginning to look a bit frayed around the edges. On the second floor, you'll find Professor Olsens Spilleland, one of the largest electronic games centres in Europe. Axeltorv is a popular meeting place for young people looking for a good time. *S and regional train: København H; bus: 1, 2, 6, 8, 13, 14, 16, 28–30, 32–34, 40, 67, 68, 69, 250 S*

## Gammeltorv and Nytorv (96/B5)

As far back as the days of the city's founder Absalon, in the middle of the 12th century, the Old Market *(Gammeltorv)* served the village of Havn, which was later to become Copenhagen, as a trading centre. Towards the eastern edge of the Gammeltorv is the *Caritas Fountain,* which was erected in the year 1608. To celebrate the birthdays of members of the Royal Family, gold-plated apples bob up and down on the jets of water, which is why the fountain has acquired the nickname, "Golden Apple Fountain". There were at one time many more apples, but they have fallen prey to those members of the community with little or no respect for the monarchy, and now there are only three or four left. The figure in the centre of the fountain, a superb piece of Renaissance work, is a beautiful, pregnant woman with a boy in her arms and one at her feet – the Copenhagen equivalent of Manneken-Pis in Brussels. Water even gushes out of the breasts of "brotherly love".

Also on the eastern side of the Gammeltorv stood the first of Copenhagen's five Town Halls; this one was destroyed in 1368. The third and fourth Town Halls stood opposite, on the New Market *(Nytorv).* The fourth was built in 1475 and gutted in the fire of 1795. Fittingly, it was here, on the site of the classical-style law courts building, where justice is dispensed to this day, that the gallows once stood.

*Eye-catching meeting point on the Gammeltorv: the Caritas Fountain*

Next to the court building was a prison, which supposedly inspired Hans Christian Andersen to write his story *The Tinderbox*. Every time he walked past, he saw a poor soldier sitting in the prison... *Bus: 5*

## Gråbrødretorv (96/C4)

★ ☼ ⚐ Cosy restaurants, garden cafés and wine bars enclose the broad Gråbrødretorv, with its cobbled surface and mighty tree – plus sculpture – in the centre. Gråbrødretorv means Greyfriar's Market or Square, a name which derives from the Franciscan monastery which was built here at the beginning of the 13th century and which today no longer exists. The carefully renovated houses on the square, their colourful façades exuding an almost Mediterranean flair, were all built either following the great fire of 1728 or in the wake of the British bombardment of the city in 1807. Guests at the restaurants *Peder Oxe* (house No. 11) and *Bøf & Ost* (No. 13) have to pass through a Romanesque vaulted cellar to reach their shared lavatories. The Gråbrødretorv is a popular meeting place for young people in particular and, in the summer, when it is at its most crowded, it's the setting for concerts and theatre productions. *S and regional train: Nørreport; bus: 5, 14, 16, 31, 42, 43, 184, 350 S*

## Kongens Nytorv (97/D-E4)

The Copenhageners have been rather unlucky with the equestrian statue of Christian V. They commissioned French sculptor Abraham-César Lamoureux to produce the monument, which was cast in lead in 1687. It turned out to be somewhat unstable and had to be supported by a figure of a naked man – "Envy", though others prefer "Jealousy" – underneath the belly of the horse. Unfortunately, this was not sufficient to prevent further contortion of the horse over the following 250 years; the left foreleg in particular resembled a less than majestic sausage, which hardly contributed to the desired image of Christian V as a Roman Emperor astride his noble steed! In short, there was nothing to be done but to re-cast the statue, but this time in bronze.

When Christian V became king, Kongens Nytorv, the King's New Square, was conceived both as a central parade ground for all branches of the military and also, on the French model, as a *place royale*, symbolising the new, absolutist power of the king. Despite groaning under the volume of traffic which crosses it daily, Kongens Nytorv still retains a majestic air, which is only impaired by the construction work on the underground railway which is currently going on. Not surprisingly it is the site of several significant buildings. It was here that Count Ulrik Frederik Gyldenløve, a half-brother to Christian V, built *Charlottenborg Palace* (Kongens Nytorv No. 1) in 1672–1683, which has been the seat of the Academy of Arts and its exhibition rooms since 1754. Here, too, is the palace of Count Thott (No. 4) which today houses the French Embassy. Number 13 is the huge, palatial department store Magasin du Nord; the building as we see it today was constructed in 1893–1894. Finally, the Royal Theatre, built in 1872–1874 and featuring numerous Renaissance elements, also graces the square. Every year, in June, the atmosphere on the Kongens Nytorv becomes more relaxed, as relieved and happy school-leavers dance around the statue of the Danish monarch. From the pre-Christmas period until well into February, a circular ice-rink is constructed around the statue, which is open until midnight (skates for rent). *Bus: 1, 6, 9, 10, 27–29, 31, 42, 43*

### Kultorvet (96/B–C3)

♁ Copenhagen's main library, housed in an unimaginative new building, completely ruins a square which is not exactly attractive in the first place, despite a number of fine, old buildings. When the sun shines, however, a certain Mediterranean atmosphere ensues, when every square metre of space inside and outside the cafés and restaurants around the square is filled with tables and chairs. Those who don't manage to get a seat, or would rather save money and bring along their own snack, just sit down on the ground, in typically Danish fashion. Children play in between the tables, street musicians accompany the goings-on with a tune and babies' cries are heard coming from their prams. *S and regional train: Nørreport; bus: 5*

## PALACES

### Amalienborg (97/F2–3)

In 1749 King Frederik V commissioned court architect Nikolai Eigtved with the building of the Frederiksstaden district, which includes the Marble Church, the Prince's Palace – now part of the National Museum – and also the marble bridge over Frederik's Canal between the Christiansborg Palace and the museum. At that time, however, he did not have suf-

ficient money to create a truly representative square which would "crown" his city. He came upon the idea of giving four noblemen the necessary land and the promise of tax exemption for decades to come. In return, they should have four palaces built according to Eigtved's plans. The four, Count Levetzau, Count Moltke, Baron Brockdorff and Privy Counsellor Løvenskjold, willingly took up the offer and by 1760 the Rococo palaces were completed. It was not long, though, before they were handed over to the Crown in 1794, since the Christiansborg Palace burnt down and the monarch was left without a roof over his head! Since then, the Amalienborg Palace – the four elements grouped around a 12-m-high equestrian statue of Frederik V on an octagonal square – has been the official residence of the Royal Family. Margrethe II lives with her consort in the Schack Palace (formerly the Løvenskjold Palace), the first building on the left, as seen from the Oslo Quay. When the Queen is in residence, the Danish flag flies above the palace and the Changing of the Guard is performed daily at midday on a larger scale than usual. The Queen Mother, Ingrid, lives in the Brockdorff Palace on the right. On the left, opposite the Schack Palace is the Moltke Palace, which is used for official functions and was recently renovated at great cost. Crown Prince Frederik and his brother Prince Joachim live in the fourth palace, the Levetzau. This was also the residence of King Christian VIII (1839–48) and King Christian X (1912–47), whose ornately furnished private apartments – for some, a little too ornate – are open to the public. In keeping with the practical and down-to-earth image of the Danish Royal Family, the Castle Square is open to traffic. Buses and lorries are prohibited, but passenger cars may pass unhindered. For security reasons, however, they are not allowed to stop on the square.

In 1983 the Danish shipping magnate A. P. Møller created the Amalien Garden *(Amaliehaven)*, a garden situated between the Amalienborg Palace and the Oslo Quay, and donated it to the general public. Admittedly, he received little thanks at first for his gesture, because he brought in artists from outside Denmark – a landscape gardener from Belgium and a sculptor from Italy – to realise his plans. The Copenhageners tended to find fault with the garden, in-

stead of using it. Even so, flagstones made of Bornholm granite were laid down and, in the meantime, the little park has achieved general acceptance. *Christian VIII's Palace (Levetzau Palace); www.kulturnet.dk/homes.rosenb; Jan.–April and Nov.–Dec.: Tues–Sun, 11 am–4 pm; closed in pre-Christmas period; May–Oct.: daily 11 am–4 pm; admission: adults: 40, children: 10 dkr; bus: 1, 6, 9, 10, 29, 650 S*

## Christiansborg     (96–97/C–D5–6)

Christiansborg Palace, the third on this site, stands on historic ground: during construction work in 1907–1928 the ruins of Bishop Absalon's medieval castle of 1167 were uncovered and restored, together with traces of the building which replaced it, Copenhagen Castle. Today, these remains can be

---

### Copenhagen: one city, one card

Whether it's the Tivoli or Carlsberg Brewery, the Ny Carlsberg Glyptotek or the National Museum, the Copenhagen Card will get you in there free. With it, you can visit around 60 attractions without paying a single Krone. In addition, the Copenhagen Card, which is issued by Copenhagen's Tourist Office "Wonderful Copenhagen", is also a bus and rail pass, which entitles the holder to free travel on all buses, high-speed (S) trains and regional trains in Greater Copenhagen. Numerous companies, for example car rental companies and sightseeing tour operators, offer card-holders substantial discounts.

The little plastic card can be purchased at all DSB stations in Greater Copenhagen, in tourist offices, Copenhagen's Tourist Information Office and many hotels. Three different cards are available: the 24-hour card costs 155 dkr, the 48-hour card costs 255 dkr and the 72-hour card costs 320 dkr. Two children under the age of five are covered by one adult card. For children of five to eleven, the three cards mentioned above are available at half price, 75, 125 and 160 dkr. Each card comes complete with a 111-page booklet containing information on opening times of the participating attractions and transport links.

viewed, underneath the present building. The new Baroque structure, Christiansborg, was built in 1733–1745 and was noted for its sumptuous furnishings. It was not even quite finished, when it burnt down in 1794. The second Christiansborg, seat of the parliament, but not a royal residence (the Royal Family had moved to Amalienborg), was built in 1803–1828. It too fell victim to a fire in 1884. Only the Palace Church, which was consecrated in 1846 and features embellishments by Bertel Thorvaldsen, managed to survive the flames. *(Open Sun, midday–4 pm; April, July and Oct.: daily midday–4 pm)*. The current building was completed in 1928 and houses the 179-seat parliament (Folketing) plus the Finance Ministry (but not the Foreign Ministry, as is often stated – this has long been situated in Christianshavn). Here, too, are function rooms for official gatherings. These somewhat over-stylised Royal Reception Rooms may also be visited as part of the guided tour. The Knights' Hall is very impressive, but Denmark can offer other, more beautiful and genuine old castles than this one. *Guided tours in English: June–Oct.: daily; Oct.–Dec.: Tues, Thurs, Sat and Sun only, 11 am, 1 pm and 3 pm; admission: adults: 40, children: 10 dkr. Ruins beneath the castle: May–Sept.: daily 9.30 am–3.30 pm; Oct.–Dec.: Tues, Thurs, Sat and Sun; Jan.–April: daily, except Mon, 9.30 am–3 pm; admission: adults: 20, children: 5 dkr; Folketing (Parliament): Guided tours in English: Oct.–Mar.: Sun, 10 am, 11 am, 1 pm, 2 pm, 3 pm and 4 pm; admission: free; Christiansborg Castle Square; www.ses.dk (ruins only); bus 1, 2, 6, 8–10, 28, 29, 31, 37, 550 S, 650 S*

The Royal Stables, known as the *Ridebane*, survived the inferno of 1794 and are a charming example of Viennese Baroque architecture. Saddle horses and carthorses are kept here in truly regal style! The stables and also the collections of uniforms, harness and carriages are open to the public (Entrance 12), as is the Royal Court Theatre which dates back to the year 1766 and can be seen today in its renovated form of 1842 (Entrance 18). No productions have been staged here since 1922, and the building serves as a theatre museum, showing costumes, original sets and models, plus numerous photographs. Visitors can savour what it feels like to tread the boards and stand in the glare of the footlights as they gaze out over the – admittedly empty – auditorium. In the mornings, it is possible to stand in the yard between the two indoor riding arenas and watch how the horses of the Royal Stables are exercised by riders or carriage-drivers and, with a bit of luck, you may be able to snatch a glimpse of today's fleet of vehicles, the royal limousines (Entrance 6). *Royal Stables and Carriage Museum: May–Sept.: Fri–Sun, 2 pm–4 pm; Oct.–April: Sat–Sun, 2 pm–4 pm; admission: adults: 10, children: 5 dkr; Theatre Museum: Wed, 2 pm–4 pm, Sat–Sun, midday–4 pm; admission: adults: 20, children: 5 dkr; Christiansborg Ridebane; bus: 1, 2, 5, 6, 8–10, 28, 29, 31, 73 E, 550 S, 650 S*

## Rosenborg     (96/C2)

★ A fairy-tale castle if ever there was one, the pretty Renaissance castle of Rosenborg stands in the flower-filled garden known as Kongens Have or Rosenborg Have, which is cherished by the Copenhageners as a much-used recreation area. Christian IV had the castle built in 1606/07 and it was considerably extended soon afterwards, in 1613–1617. The striking octagonal tower which houses a spiral staircase was added twenty years later. Originally standing far beyond the city's fortified boundary, the castle served until the middle of the 18th century as a summer residence, then seemed to be forgotten and was only used as storage space by the royal household. In this way, many items of silver furniture were preserved which would otherwise most probably have been melted down once they had gone out of fashion! These include serving tables which could be filled with hot water to keep food warm prior

*Summer residence, storeroom, museum – Rosenborg Castle*

to serving and statuettes of dogs, also filled in this way to serve as a source of heat.

Most of these pieces are to be found in the impressive Knights' Hall on the first floor. Recently, the Gobelin tapestries have been returned, which Christian V had woven in 1685 especially for the Hall – and which have adorned the Knights' Hall at the Christiansborg Palace since 1927. Among the 24 rooms, some of which boast their original furnishings, is also Christian IV's study.

Since 1975 the cellar underneath the castle has housed the Treasure Chamber, which contains the imperial regalia, including the priceless crown which, for 170 years from 1670, symbolised the absolute power of the Danish monarchy. *May–Sept.: daily 10 am–4 pm; Oct.: daily 11 am–3 pm; Nov.–April: daily, except Mon, 11 am–2 pm; admission: adults: 45, children: 10 dkr; www. kulturnet.dk /homes.rosenb; S and regional train: Nørreport; bus: 5, 10, 14, 16, 31, 42, 43, 184, 185, 350 S*

## STREETS

### Nyhavn (97/E–F 4)

★ At one time the branch canal which Christian V had dug in 1673 to link the harbour with Kongens Nytorv had a less-than-respectable side (odd house numbers) and a respectable side (even numbers)! These days, though, the former has assumed the mantle of respectability and the sailors' bars have all but disappeared, except for a few which have been polished up for the tourists. As a re-

*Maritime atmosphere on the Nyhavn branch canal*

sult, much of the infrastructure associated with such a dubious harbour area has also vanished. Today this side is a pedestrian zone with expensive, mainly typically cosy Danish restaurants. Weather permitting, diners sit outside on the terraces at the water's edge. If required, a warming blanket for the knees is also part of the service. Everyone enjoys the view across to the floating museums at anchor – only wooden vessels are allowed to put into Nyhavn – and to the "respectable" other side. It was on this side that Hans Christian Andersen lived on two occasions, in house No. 20 and house No. 60. The oldest house on the Nyhavn, No. 9, has stood since 1681 and gives you some impression of the typical housing prior to the fire of 1728.

### Pistolstræde                    (97/D4)

It's not exactly a street, more a lane really, shaped like a pistol and leading from the Østergade to the Ny Østergade. At one time, the houses to the rear were on the point of being knocked down, but then several shops and restaurants re-discovered this idyllic alleyway as a good place to do business.

### Strøget          (96–97/B–D4–5)

★ ☺ Strøget is a shopping street, its 1.8 km making it supposedly the longest in Europe. On the occasion of Copenhagen's 800th birthday party, the longest breakfast buffet in the world was set up here. To be fair, the Strøget actually a chain of five streets, running from the Town Hall Square towards Kongens Nytorv; Frederiksberggade, Ny-

gade, Vimmelskaftet, Amagertorv and Østergade. Whereas in the Frederiksberggade cheap tourist shops and bars abound, the part of the Strøget between Amagertorv and Kongens Nytorv has been dubbed by the locals the "royal end".

## DISTRICTS

### Christiania                   (105/E4)

⚑ Christiania lies in the Christianshavn district and is even more colourful than its namesake. For thirty years now, the residents have been practising an alternative lifestyle. Visitors are welcome at the cafés and restaurants or to come and listen to a concert in the Free City of Christiania. On the other hand, the sight of hordes of tourists armed with cameras, on the lookout for snapshots as they roam the streets of this former military site, doesn't go down well.

### Christianshavn                 (97/F6)

★ A hint of Amsterdam is in the air in the Christianshavn district which was established on the island of Amager by King Christian IV from 1618 onwards. Canals criss-cross this quarter and the roads run at right angles to one another. Christianshavn was spared the fate of other parts of the city, which were devastated by fire over the centuries. Consequently many of the original houses have survived to the present day. Some are a little down-at-heel, others painted in cheerful colours and those on the canal have a boat moored at the front door.

## Frederiksberg (102/C4)

Frederiksberg is not a district of Copenhagen, but an independent commune with around 85,000 inhabitants, who are proud of their independence, not least because their community is richer than impoverished Copenhagen. A huge Town Hall (1949–1953) and the Falkoner Center, which is used for congresses and exhibitions, seem to epitomise the sense of superiority felt by the Frederiksbergers.

At the weekend the Copenhageners come out to stroll around in the park surrounding Frederiksberg Castle, the ★ ✺ *Frederiksberg Have.* The summer residence built around 1700 is now home to a military academy and is not open to the public. The image of a bull adorns the tympanum of the little Apis temple in the castle grounds, designed in 1802–1804 by Danish painter Nicolai Abildgaard. It was inspired by a Roman temple which was dedicated to Apis, the sacred bull worshiped by the Ancient Egyptians. At one time, the temple was used as an entrance to the neighbouring zoo. On one of the islands in the romantic network of canals which runs through the park stands a Chinese Tea House. In 18th-century Europe it was fashionable among the nobility to show an interest in Chinese culture. Today, young Copenhageners are "in" if they choose to get married underneath one of the trees in the park. The celebrations begin with punting on the canals and continue in one of the *Små Have (Small Gardens)* which lie on the outskirts of the park, along the Pile Allé. The park also boasts three almost identical family beer gardens, none of which has changed much in the last hundred years. They are only open in summer and are relatively little known among tourists. To make up for this, you'll find many more Copenhageners here, having a really good time – at weekends, there's music too. *Admission: free; Roskildevej/ Pile Allé; bus: 6, 18, 28, 550 S*

## Latinerkvarteret (96/A–B5)

⚡ Hardly any students live in this old university district now, which even in its heyday bore no resemblance whatsoever to the Latin Quarter in Paris. It lies between Vestervoldgade (the part between Jarmers Plads and Rådhuspladsen) and Fiolstræde with the Frue Plads at its heart. There are various old university buildings here and many book shops. The majority of the university institutes have moved to Amager. The Latin Quarter distinguishes itself from other parts of Copenhagen by its countless cheap shops, pizzerias, snack bars and a colourful café and club scene.

## Nørrebro (100/A–B5–6, 103/E–F1, 104/A–B1)

✺ ⚡ Over the last few years, more and more young people in particular are moving out of the centre of Copenhagen. Here, in the Nørrebro district, and round the Skt. Hans Torv in particular, a colourful, multi-cultural alternative scene has developed, including cafés, music bars and small shops, notably junk shops. Many students live here and the proportion of foreigners amongst the residents is particularly high. Everything is cheaper here than in the city centre and consequently less well looked-after.

## Nyboder      (97/E1)

In 1631, in order to discourage seamen from signing up on foreign ships simply because they could find nowhere to live in Copenhagen, Christian IV set up Nyboder, a kind of subsidised residential area. It lies between the Marble Church and the park at the Citadel. In Skt. Pauls Gade you can still find a few of the original, colourful half-timbered houses.

## Vesterbro      (103/E–F3–6)

The term "red-light district" does not accurately describe the part of Vesterbro between the station, Vesterbrogade and the railway lines, with the Istedgade as the main thoroughfare running across it towards the west. In this part of what used to be a working-class district, you will find many small, reasonably priced shops and numerous foreign restaurants alongside the sex shops. Cultural needs are catered for at the new culture centre, Øksnehallen, located in a former fish auctioneer's which dates back to 1901. Regular exhibitions, events and conferences are held – all with a whiff of the *avant-garde* to them.

Also worth a visit is the pool and the health and fitness centre in the huge *Vandkulturhuset*, which is part of the equally huge *DGI-byen* with its sports facilities, restaurants and hotel. *Øksnehallen, Halmtorvet 11; Tel. 33 86 04 00; www.oeksnehallen.dk; Vandkulturhuset, Tietgensgade 65; Tel. 33 29 81 00; www.dgibyen.dk*

*No trip to Copenhagen is complete without a visit to The Little Mermaid*

## The Little Mermaid      (101/E6)

Surprisingly few of the tourists who make their way everyday along the Langelinie promenade to see The Little Mermaid *(Den lille Havfrue)* actually know Hans Christian Andersen's heartrending fairy story about the unrequited love of the 15-year-old mermaid for a young human prince. The bronze statue, created in 1913 by Danish sculptor Edvard Eriksen, is smaller than you would probably expect and sits on a rock just a few steps from the bank in shallow water. The fact that the figure has neither a proper fishes' tail or a pair of human legs is a reference to the fairy story, in which the mermaid sacrifices her sweet voice in order to exchange the former for the latter! *Langelinie; bus: 1, 6, 9*

# Two hours in a museum

*Copenhagen can boast only a few world-class museums,
but those it has should not be missed*

There are in excess of sixty museums in and around Copenhagen, and the number increases year by year. All are conceived and laid out in true Danish style: visitor-oriented, tasteful and somehow *hyggelig,* that is, welcoming and cosy. Despite the fact that only a few really stand up to international competition, they are all ideal for passing a couple of hours on a rainy day. Take for example the *Believe it or Not,* in which curious items from all over the world have been assembled (genuine or fake, take your pick) or the *Guinness World of Records Museum* and the *Louis Tussaud's Wax Museum* (in the latter, only the chamber of horrors is a little over the top!). On the other hand, though, you are not missing much if you choose not to go in.

Museums of truly international stature are rare in Copenhagen. The National Museum is one of them, so too are the Ny Carlsberg Glyptotek, the National Gallery and – we strongly advise you not to miss this one – the Louisiana Museum of Modern Art in Humlebæk, to the

*The Ny Carlsberg Glyptotek*

north of Copenhagen. These are backed up by a broad range of respectable collections which are well worth a visit, if not on this trip to the city, then on your next.

As is the case in many other cities, the majority of museums are closed on Mondays, a fact which has annoyed residents and visitors alike for years. The admission fees are moderately high, but if you have a Copenhagen Card, you can often get in for free.

### Arken                                              (U/D6)

★ Søren Robert Lund was still an architecture student when he produced the winning design for the Arken Museum (The Ark) in Ishøj, to the south of Copenhagen. He has created one of the most spectacular museum buildings of the present day. A daring structure, reminiscent of a ship's hull, rises up over the bay of Køge. Inside, the ship motif is picked up repeatedly, notably in the 150-m-long "Axis of Art", the main hall, which has one straight and one curved side, creating the most fascinating optical effects. The "Museum of Modern Art" with its changing exhibitions,

# MARCO POLO SELECTION: MUSEUMS

**1  Arken**
It's more the architecture than the contemporary art which draws the crowds to the "Ark" at Ishøj (page 35)

**2  Experimentarium**
Hands-on fun with the laws of nature (page 36)

**3  Frihedsmuseet**
Resistance museum – unique and unprecedented (page 37)

**4  Karen Blixen Museet**
At home with Denmark's great female writer (page 38)

**5  Louisiana**
Art, architecture and landscape in total harmony (page 40)

**6  Nationalmuseet**
Three museums in one – plus one for the kids (page 41)

**7  Ny Carlsberg Glyptotek**
From antiquity to the "Golden Age": a world-class collection right across the board (page 42)

**8  Statens Museum for Kunst**
The National Gallery whose extension is a work of art in itself (page 44)

unites all manner of artistic activity under one roof. *Tues–Sun, 10 am–5 pm; admission: adults: 40, children: 15 dkr; Ishøj coastal park, Skovvej 100; www.arken.dk; S: Ishøj; bus: 128*

### Experimentarium (U/E4)

★ In a disused warehouse belonging to the Tuborg Brewery, spread over 4,000 sq m, is a scientific exhibition with a difference. Here, the visitor can get real hands-on experience of science in action. Sixteen thematic zones, covering such topics as "Focus on light", "Atoms and radiation" or "How the body works", invite you to perform over 250 experiments yourself. For instance, you might like to communicate with a satellite via a weather computer, subject yourself to a lie-detector test or send a whispered greeting to a loved-one over a distance of 50 m with the aid of a parabolic mirror.

To get the most out of the experience, visitors should be at least nine years old. This doesn't mean to say that the very young scientists have been completely forgotten; they can experiment in a water play area with pumps, sluices and ships. Written instructions accompanying the experiments are in Danish, Swedish and English and friendly staff are on hand to explain further if necessary. *Jan.–mid-June, mid-Aug.–Dec.: Mon, Wed–Fri, 9 am–5 pm, Tues, 9 am–9 pm, Sat–Sun, 11 am–5 pm; mid-June–mid-Aug.: daily 10 am–5 pm; admission: adults: 79, children 57 dkr; Tuborg Havnevej 7, Hellerup; www.experimentarium.dk; S: Svanemøllen; bus: 6, 21, 650 S*

## Frederiksborg (U/C2)

It is well worth making the 35-km journey to Hillerød, to the north-west of Copenhagen, to visit the castle-cum-museum of Frederiksborg. The impressive Renaissance castle stands in a picturesque setting on an island in the middle of a lake. Christian IV had this magnificent estate built between 1602 and 1620. Without much ado, he demolished the previous castle, built by his father. The audience chamber and imposing Knights' Hall are of particular interest. The church, in which from 1671 onwards the Danish kings were crowned and anointed, is situated in the same wing. The interior features a very fine silver altar and a small organ built in 1610 by Esaias Compenius. The last king to receive the royal insignia here was Christian VIII in 1840. Frederiksborg was, by this time, seldom used as an official residence by the Danish kings, as it had been by Christian IV, his son Frederik III and his grandson Christian V. Nearby Fredensborg, built by Frederik IV in 1720, took over the role of favourite residence, and to this day, is the palace in which the Danish royal family chooses to spend the spring and autumn. It was Frederik VII who alone preferred Frederiksborg to the other royal palaces and made this spacious castle his home. He was even present in December 1859, when most of the palace complex – with the exception of the church and the audience chambers (in a separate building) – was destroyed by fire. Once again, it was the founder of the Carlsberg Brewery, J. C. Jacobsen, who initiated the rebuilding of the castle.

It was his desire, though, that the castle no longer serve as a royal residence, but should be turned into a museum. Frederiksborg therefore also bears the title Museum of National History and includes paintings, furniture and crafts from the last 500 years. *Nov.–Mar.: daily 11 am–3 pm; April and Oct.: daily 10 am–5 pm; admission: adults: 45, children: 10 dkr; Hillerød; www .frederiks borg museet. dk; S: Hillerød; bus: 325, 701–703*

## Frihedsmuseet (105/E1)

★ The Danish Resistance Museum has recently been renovated and its didactic concept improved. It is dedicated to the fight for freedom of the Danish people from 1940–1945, and is unique in the world for its dramatic and detailed illustration of the struggle of a nation against an occupying regime. The material on display was originally put together for a one-off exhibition, and documents the sabotage activities by Danish resistance workers, the provision of supplies and reinforcements from Great Britain and the work of the underground press. Part of the exhibition is devoted to showing how it was possible to save Danish Jews from the Nazis, by first hiding them and then smuggling them out of the country and into neutral Sweden. *Mid-Sept.–April: Tues–Sat, 11 am–3 pm, Sun, 11 am–4 pm; May–mid-Sept.: Tues–Sat, 10 am–4 pm, Sun, 10 am–5 pm; admission: free; Churchill parken; www.natmus.dk; S and regional train: Østerport; bus: 1, 6, 9, 19, 29*

## Gammel Dok (97/E5)

Not a museum as such, but rather a group of exhibition rooms, this renovated 18th-century storehouse stands directly on the quay at Christianshavn. Gammel Dok offers a unique backdrop, not only for changing exhibitions (often more than one at any one time) dedicated to Danish architecture – the central theme underlying each Gammel Dok presentation – but also stages special events, featuring the design and art industries in Denmark. *Daily 10 am–5 pm; admission: adults: 30 dkr, children: free; Strandgade 27 B; www.kulturnet.dk; bus: 31, 32, 350 S*

## Den Hirschsprungske Samling (96/C1)

Although the Skagen painters achieved a certain degree of world-wide fame, Danish art of the 19th and 20th centuries is generally underestimated, even among art lovers. That is, of course, until they have taken a closer look at the Hirschsprung Collection. It was painstakingly put together over a period of 40 years by a tobacco manufacturer, Heinrich Hirschsprung (1836–1908) and his wife Pauline. Hirschsprung bequeathed to the Danish state the works of art, and the small museum built in a charming park to house them. The collection, opened to the general public in 1911, focuses on the so-called "Golden Age" of Danish art, and features works by such painters as Christoffer Wilhelm Eckersberg, Christen Købke and Johan Thomas Lundbye. The Skagen artists are represented by Anna and Michael Ancher, Peter Severin Krøyer and Christian Krohg. Works by eminent artists such as Vilhelm Hammershøj and Kristian Zahrtmann are naturally also on display. The paintings are hung relatively close together and the individual rooms are furnished with contemporary furniture – some of which was designed by the artists themselves. These facts go to make such an intimate atmosphere within this small museum, that you almost feel you are paying a visit to one or other of the artists at home. *Thurs–Mon, 11 am–4 pm, Wed, 11 am–9 pm; closed Tues; admission: adults: 25 dkr, children: free; Stockholmsgade 20; www.kultur net. dk/homes/hirs; S: Østerport; bus: 10, 14, 40, 42, 43, 184, 185*

## Karen Blixen Museet (U/E3)

★ This enchanting museum leaves the visitor guessing about one thing: why did Karen Blixen give herself the Christian name Tania for her German readers, while the rest of the world knew her by the name of Karen? Approximately 25 km to the north of Copenhagen is Rungsted, and here, on the Rung-

---

### In the spirit of Marco Polo

Marco Polo was the first true world traveller. He travelled with peaceful intentions forging links between the East and the West. His aim was to discover the world, and explore different cultures and environments without changing or disrupting them. He is an excellent role model for the travellers of today and the future. Wherever we travel we should show respect for other peoples and the natural world.

stedlund estate, is the small museum which you really should not miss. The writer Karen Blixen (1885–1962) returned here to her parents' home in 1931, following her stay in Kenya, and remained here until her death. Most of her more famous books were written on the small Corona typewriter, which was her constant companion. It is here, of course, along with her last fountain pen, photographs illustrating her life and many, many books. A slide show consisting of 80 black and white slides (and accompanied by a commentary in Danish and English) conveys a truer and more vivid picture of Karen Blixen's time in Africa from 1914 to 1931 than the cinema film *Out of Africa* managed to do. After visiting the exhibition rooms, which are located in a former storehouse in Rungstedlund, visitors are allowed, in small groups, to take a look at the writer's private flat. Each group has twenty minutes in which to savour the atmosphere of these rooms which have been left just as they were when Blixen was still alive. You can't help feeling that she will walk into the room at any minute to welcome her guests in person! The illusion is perfect, right down to the last detail: bunches of her favourite wild flowers adorn the room and the net curtains which she brought back from her farm in Kenya still hang – much too long for the rooms here in Rungstedlund, with their lower ceilings – the material lying in great folds on the floor. In one corner stands the gramophone, given to her by her lover Denys Finch Hatton, just before his plane crashed in the mountains.

A 16-hectare area of parkland on the Rungstedlund estate has today been set aside as a *bird sanctuary*. It is open to the public and is a favourite spot for a picnic among the Danes. Karen Blixen lies buried here, underneath a large beech tree. *May–Sept.: daily 10 am–5 pm; Oct.–April: Wed–Fri, 1 pm–4 pm, Sat–Sun, 11 am–4 pm; admission: adults: 33 dkr, children: free; Rungsted Strandvej 111; www.isak-dinesen.dk; regional train: Rungsted Kyst; bus: 388*

### Københavns Bymuseet (103/F4)

In the summer, a ceramic model of medieval Copenhagen graces the garden in front of the Copenhagen City Museum – a must for all those who wish to discover more about the history of the city and its citizens. The museum is located in a dignified setting, a building dating back to the end of the 18th century which used to house the Royal Shooting Range of the local shooting club. The finest exhibits are actually outside the museum in the neighbouring Absalonsgade – benches and street lights, a fire alarm and a kiosk, all from the period from 1860 to 1935. Each well-labelled item helps to illustrate the development from late Classicism through Historicism and *Art nouveau* down to Functionalism. The road itself, with its cobblestones and gutters, is designed to suggest a typical city street of a century ago. *May–Sept: Wed–Mon, 10 am–4 pm; Oct–April: Wed–Mon, 1 pm–4 pm; admission: free; Vesterbrogade 59; www.kbhbmuseum.dk; bus: 16, 28, 550 S*

### Kunstindustriemuseet (105/E2)

The arts and crafts museum, founded in 1890, is housed in a former hospital dating back to the

18th century – a rather makeshift solution, given the quality of the exhibits. The rooms are simply too big to allow suitable presentation of the treasures which have been gathered together, the subdivision of rooms appears to be only of a temporary nature. It is particularly noticeable that, unlike most Danish museums, the didactic quality of this otherwise noteworthy exhibition leaves a lot to be desired. The collection spans European arts and crafts from the Middle Ages to the present day, plus Chinese and Japanese items. The range of modern design objects is disappointingly meagre. *Tues–Fri, 10 am–4 pm, Sat–Sun, midday–4 pm (parts of the collection are only open to the public on all days from midday–4 pm); admission: adults: 35 dkr, children: free; Bredgade 68; www.mus-kim.dk; S: Østerport; bus: 1, 6, 9, 29*

## Louisiana (U/E2)

★ A startlingly different setting for Alberto Giacometti's spindly sculptures: one wall of this specially-commissioned exhibition room is made entirely of glass. The contrast between the sculptures and their backdrop of trees in the park which surrounds the museum is quite stunning. Alexander Calder's giant mobile sculptures are perceived in quite a different light against the panorama of the Øresund and the Swedish coast behind them. Such dramatic contrasts of vision and perspective are fundamental to the artistic concept of the Louisiana Museum of Modern Art. Here, art, architecture and landscape fuse together into one. Louisiana lies 30 km north of Copenhagen in Humlebæk.

Founder and driving force behind the museum is Knud W. Jensen, who is also its current director. In two stages, between 1958 and 1991, this modern museum building was constructed adjacent to an old manor house, whereby care was taken to incorporate the sloping terrain and the park-like landscape into the overall presentation concept. Denmark's most-visited museum exudes an agreeably relaxed atmosphere in which to marvel at a seemingly inexhaustible wealth of contemporary pieces. The collection covers the period from the end of World War II to the present day, and encompasses works by, among others, Vasarély, Dewasne, Albers and Bill. International artistic trends of the 1960s, 1970s and 1980s are illustrated by Tinguely, César and Klein. Warhol, Dine, Rauschenberg, Lichtenstein and Oldenburg represent the pop art movement; Beuys is here, so too are Baselitz, Kienholz and Kiefer – as you can see, a wide and comprehensive spectrum. The museum's collection of graphics is also worthy of note. It is housed in a new wing of the building. In addition, Louisiana stages between eight and ten special exhibitions each year, every one of them worth a visit in its own right. Three points of interest on your tour of the museum deserve particular attention. Firstly the above-mentioned Giacometti Room with its huge window-wall; secondly the room in the south wing, lit only by artificial light, in which a motor-driven sculpture by Tinguely perches precariously in front of a mammoth work by Roy Lichtenstein. Finally, don't forget the en-

*Louisiana gives you a new perspective on things*

chanting corner of the sprawling park, where sculptures by Hans Arp and Henry Moore harmonise so well with the natural surroundings, that it is as if they have always been here. If your head is spinning from so many visual impressions, you can relax in the museum café – in fine weather, sitting out on the terrace, where you can fully appreciate the interplay of architecture and landscape. A very special attraction at the museum is the *Children's House,* in which visitors at the lower end of the age spectrum can learn more about the creative processes behind the exhibits, in a playful atmosphere and helped by the patient and expert museum staff. There's plenty of room to play, too. *Daily 10 am–5 pm (Wed, until 10 pm); admission: adults: 60, children: 15 dkr; Gammel Strandvej 13, Humlebæk; www.louisiana.dk; regional train: Humlebæk and bus no. 388 (or ten minutes on foot)*

## Nationalmuseet (96/C6)

★ You could spend several days exploring the National Museum. Its name stands not only for Denmark's foremost museum in the field of cultural history, but also for a noteworthy collection of ethnological exhibits and classical antiquities. The heart of the museum is the Prince's Palace, built in 1684, which has been enhanced by several extensions since the opening of the museum in 1807, and now takes up an entire block in the centre of Copenhagen. The most recent addition was made in 1992, in the course of which the overall layout of the various collections and the didactic concept behind them was reworked.

The cultural history collection, which documents life in Denmark from the Stone Age to the present day, is divided into three parts. The section of pre- and early history (1300 BC–1000 AD) presents finds from the Stone Age, Bronze and Iron Ages and from the Viking era. Here you will find those famous horned helmets, normally attributed to the Vikings, although they actually date back to the Bronze Age. Replicas of Viking jewellery can be purchased at the museum shop. The next section is devoted to Denmark in the Middle Ages and the Renaissance (1000–1600 AD) and deals with the following areas: the Church in the early Middle Ages, the Scandinavians on Greenland, society and everyday life and, finally, altars and sacred silver of the Renaissance. Special displays and, above all, reconstructed interiors, give an insight into the period from 1660 to 1830. The museum also boasts one of the largest ethnographic collections in the world, with artefacts and treasures illustrating the life and culture of non-European peoples, most notably the Eskimos. The Royal Coin and Medal Collection shows principally Ancient Greek and Roman coins, coins from the Middle Ages but also from more recent times. The antiquities collection includes archaeological finds from Greece, Italy and the Middle East. Perhaps the most beautiful exhibit in the entire museum is the "sun chariot" which was discovered in Trundholm and dates back to around 1000 BC.

Although the collections are well-organised from a didactic point of view, with labels and explanatory texts in Danish and English, children could find it difficult to reap the full benefits of a visit to the museum without some sort of expert guidance. The National Museum has therefore set up a *Children's Museum*, in which all the exhibits – for the most part replicas – can be touched and actively used. Young visitors can dress up in historical costumes, experience a history lesson in a turn-of-the-century Danish classroom or be transported to a Viking trading post or medieval Danish castle. *Tues–Sun, 10 am–5 pm; admission: adults: 40 dkr, children: free; Nyvestergade 10; www.natmus.dk; bus: 1, 2, 5, 6, 8, 10, 28–30, 32, 33, 550 S, 650 S*

## Ny Carlsberg Glyptotek  (96/B6)

★ A glyptographic collection is first and foremost a collection of cut stones, hence the Ny Carlsberg Glyptotek was originally a sculpture museum. Since its founding in 1897, the museum's stock of treasures has been systematically enlarged to include a world-famous collection of paintings. The Ny Carlsberg Glyptotek consists of three museums. Carl Jacobsen (son of the founder of the Carlsberg Brewery) and his wife Ottilia decided, in 1888, to make available to a wider audience their comprehensive collection of works by Thorvaldsen pupils, contemporary artists and a number of finds from antiquity.

For this purpose, Vilhelm Dahlerup designed the older wing of the Ny Carlsberg Glyptotek, which was opened in 1897. Today, it houses the more modern pieces, while the antiquities are now in the new wing, added by Hack Kampmanns in 1906. Since then, the collection has been considerably extended in both fields. The antiquities include not only Egyptian, Greek and Roman works; the Glyptothek can claim one of the largest collections of Etruscan artefacts outside Italy. The museum is also particularly proud of its group of Rodin sculptures, one of the finest outside France. In addition, this is the most important museum in Denmark in the field of Danish sculpture since Bertel Thorvaldsen (1768–1844). Alongside the Hirschsprung Collection and the Statens Museum of Art, the Ny Carlsberg Glyptotek presents the city's third largest collection of works by painters belonging to the recently rediscovered "Golden Age", such as Christoffer Vilhelm Eckersberg, Christen Schjellerup Købke and Johan Thomas Lundbye. The two wings of the museum are linked by a room which the brochures call simply the Conservatory. This is somewhat of an understatement; it is rather a giant hall, filled with palms and other plants, with its own fountain and fish pond and is the showcase for a group of modern sculptures, among them the *Water Mother* by Kai Nielsen, a reclining figure smothered by a dozen babies. The Conservatory also features an artificially-induced, Mediterranean-type climate – intended to simulate conditions in the countries of origin of most of the works on display. Sitting here in the warm air, listening to the special sound and tone effects in the background, is an unforgettable part of any visit to the Ny Carlsberg Glyptotek. Unfortunately, the peace and quiet is often disturbed by the guests at the café which adjoins the Conservatory – not a very clever choice of location. A glass arcade leads from the Conservatory to the third wing of the museum, the three-storey new building added by Danish architect Hennig Larsen to mark Copenhagen's role as European City of Culture in 1996. This section of the museum is devoted entirely to French artists; the spectrum reaches from David to Corot and Manet on the ground floor, while the major Impressionists have the first floor to themselves, and the Post Impressionists are to be found on the second floor, including 35 works by Gauguin alone. Museum founder Carl Jacobsen was not a particular devotee of Impressionism. It was his son, Helge, who laid the foundations of this famous collection, beginning in 1915. Here, too, are all of Degas' bronze sculptures, (only one of three locations in the world where they can be viewed together), including the famous little dancer, with her leg stretched forward, her snub nose pointing into the air and the tulle skirt. The statuettes by Honoré Daumier – political caricatures cast in bronze – are surprisingly powerful and expressive. *Daily, except Mon, 10 am–4 pm; admission: adults: 30 dkr, children: free; Wed and*

43

*See the "Golden Age" revival at the National Gallery*

*Sun: free admission; Dantes Plads 7; www.glyptotek.dk; S and regional train: København H; bus: 1, 2, 5, 6, 8, 10, 28–30, 32, 33, 550 S, 650 S*

**Ordrupgaardsamlingen** (U/E4)
An important collection of French Impressionist works has been taking shape on the quiet in a small museum in Charlottenlund on the northern outskirts of Copenhagen. Major works by Manet, Renoir, Pissarro, Sisley, Monet, Gauguin and Degas are all on display here. Pictures by Danish artists

of the 19th and 20th centuries are also well able to hold their own in such illustrious company. *May–Dec: daily, except Mon, 1 pm–5 pm; Jan.–April: Tues–Fri, 1 pm–5 pm, Sat–Sun, 11 am–5 pm; admission: adults: 25 dkr, children: free; Charlottenlund, Vilvordevej 110; S: Klampenborg/Lyngby and bus 388*

**Statens Museum for Kunst (National Gallery)** (96/C1)
★ Here they are again, the painters of the "Golden Age", the Skagen and Fyn painters, classics, such

as Zahrtmann and more modern Danes, for example, Edvard Weie, Karl Isakson, Olaf Rude and Oluf Høst. The Danish National Gallery clearly puts part of its emphasis on Denmark. The significant works of the old masters on display here once formed part of the Royal collection, which laid the foundation of the Statens Museum collection. Dutch and Flemish paintings also feature strongly (although some people doubt whether four Rembrandt paintings in the collection are in fact genuine), as does French painting of the first half of the 20th century. The Statens Museum can boast 25 paintings by Henri Matisse alone, including *Le Luxe, II* from 1907/08, a major example of Fauvism. The nine magnificent Emil Nolde paintings were a gift to the museum from the painter himself. Autumn 1998 saw the opening of a new modern extension to the museum which is hardly visible from the front of the historic main building. The museum has thus almost doubled its available exhibition area. The new building, from which the visitor is allowed frequent glimpses of the park behind the museum, is devoted to contemporary art. It is itself a much-admired work of art, offering as it does an enticing contrast to the old structure. Old and new are joined by a covered inner courtyard and glass-walled passageways. *Tues and Thurs–Sun, 10 am–4.30 pm, Wed, 10 am–9 pm; admission: adults: 40 dkr, children: free; Sølvgade 48–50; www.smk.dk; S Nørreport or Østerport; bus: 10, 14, 40, 42, 43, 72 E, 173 E, 184*

## Thorvaldsens Museet (96/C5)

This magnificent building on the Castle Island, Slotsholmen, is not just a museum, it is also a mausoleum; Bertel Thorvaldsen's grave lies in the inner courtyard. Thorvaldsen (1768–1844) gave his approval to the plans drawn up by Gottlieb Bindesbøll for this monumental structure, and building work commenced while he was still alive, in the year 1839. Completed in 1848, it contains Thorvaldsen's private collection of ancient Egyptian, Greek and Roman art treasures plus a collection of paintings by contemporary Danish and European artists. The museum was conceived as a setting for Thorvaldsen's marble sculptures, including *Ganymede* and *Shepherd Boy*. This very smooth style is not to everyone's taste, perhaps, but Bertel Thorvaldsen's reputation as one of the foremost neoclassical sculptors in Denmark and beyond is unchallenged. *Tues–Sun, 10 am–5 pm; admission: adults: 20 dkr., children: free; Porthusgade 2; www.thorvaldsensmuseum.dk; bus: 1, 2, 5, 6, 8, 10, 28, 29, 550 S, 650 S*

## Tøjhusmuseet (96/C5)

The Danish Defence Museum (Dansk Forsvarsmuseum) is housed in the arsenal which was built by Christian IV towards the end of the 16th century. The 163-m-long cannon hall on the ground floor is the longest vaulted hall in Europe. The armoury on the first floor contains a display of uniforms and armour. The museum is not one of the most attractive of its kind. *Tues–Sun, midday–4 pm; admission: adults: 20, children: 5 dkr; Tøjhusgade 3; www.thm.dk; bus: 1, 2, 5, 6, 8–10, 28, 29, 31, 37, 550 S, 650 S*

# Where to dine

*Copenhagen is famous for its open sandwiches. Traditional Danish fare is also to be had in several gourmet restaurants*

The restaurant scene in Denmark as a whole and Copenhagen in particular has changed in recent years, imperceptibly at first, but with lasting effect. It has become easier for the Copenhagen visitor to find top-class restaurants (whereby prices are not always an indicator of quality). Michelin stars are being awarded more often these days.

In addition, there is a whole range of places to eat offering down-to-earth, quality Danish cooking which will also appeal to the more demanding customer. Here you can expect good, substantial portions and, occasionally, flavour combinations which are unfamiliar to the non-Danish palate, such as fish with a sweet sauce. Danish cuisine won't take you by storm, but rather talk you over gradually, if you give it the chance!

The day gets off to a good start. Breakfast, known as *morgenmad* is served in most hotels in portions which are generous to positively gargantuan. Buffets offering a wide range of dishes from sweet to healthy – you don't have to try the sweet herrings – are the order of the day. The Danes call their lunch *frokost*, which also means breakfast. At lunchtime, between midday and 2 pm – or even as late as 3 pm – the cafés and restaurants often serve a cold snack. It consists generally of the so-called *smørrebrød*, which, in translation, means "buttered bread", although it's a far cry from simple bread and butter. There are even restaurants which serve nothing but *smørrebrød* (and the corresponding alcoholic drinks to go with it). Originally intended as a snack between meals, one or two *smørrebrød* are generally sufficient to see you through the day. Large *frokost* buffets are becoming increasingly popular, for which any self-respecting Dane is willing to sacrifice two hours of his time. Such a spread also includes warm dishes. The cold evening meal is called *aftensmad*, and – just to confuse things – the warm evening meal, which is taken between 6 pm and 8 pm, is known as *middag* in Danish, which means "midday" or "midday meal"! This is when

*The restaurants and bars on Nyhavn are also popular with Copenhageners – an ideal combination of fresh air and picturesque setting on the canal*

the à la carte restaurants come into their own, where the food not only tastes good, but is presented with the typical flair of a nation famous for its designers. Restaurants generally expect their guests relatively early; 7.30 pm is about the right time to dine, since most kitchens close at around 10 pm. Take note: many restaurants do not open on Sundays!

Local beer *(øl)* is of good quality in Denmark, but is often expensive in restaurants. To go with it, the Danes like nothing better than a glass of akvavit, their famous schnapps made with caraway seeds. In recent years, more Gammel Dansk, a type of bitters, is being consumed. Out on the town, the Copenhageners are great wine drinkers; the selection of available wines and their quality has improved and prices are reasonable.

The dessert to end all desserts is called in Danish *rødgrød med fløde*, which is a kind of red fruit jelly with cream. Don't bother trying to order this delicacy yourself, unless your Danish is pretty good – its pronunciation is beyond most non-Danes!

And then there's the story of the "coffee-punch", Danish style, which is fun, but only if prepared at the table. Here, a krone coin is placed in the bottom of a coffee cup and coffee added until the coin can no longer be seen. Then the cup is topped up with akvavit, until the coin reappears. Cheers!

The A to Z of restaurants in Copenhagen goes from "A Hereford Beefstouw" to "Zorbas" – in total around 350, including cafés, though there is no clear distinction between restaurant and café in Copenhagen. Many cafés, which are often more reminiscent of a small bistro than of a Viennese coffee house, serve excellent meals – and offer live music in the evenings to boot.

## CAFÉS

### Amokka (100/C5)

★ ◁◁ Situated just a stone's throw from the city centre, this bright café, a little on the chic side, claims to be "heaven on earth" for coffee lovers. It certainly has the prettiest terrace in town, with a view across the Sortedams Sø on the other side of the road, to justify its claim. In-house coffee creations can be bought in the little coffee shop and there's brunch on offer at the weekend. *Coffee tasting: Mon–Fri, 6 pm. Open, Mon–Fri, 8 am–midnight, Sat, 9 am–midnight, Sun, 10 am–10 pm; Dag Hammerskjölds Allé 38–40 (on the Lille Triangle Plads)*

### Café Dan Turrell (97/D3)

Named after the – now deceased – writer and *bon viveur*, who still enjoys immense popularity in Denmark. Bright, *avant-garde* atmosphere, mixed clientele, not expensive. In the evenings there are literary readings and live music performances (jazz). *Mon–Tues, 9 am –midnight, Wed, 9 am–1 am, Thurs, 9 am–2 am, Fri, 9 am–4 am, Sat, 11 am–4 am, Sun, 11 am–midnight; Store Regnegade 3–5*

### Café Europa (96/C4)

🏃 Modern café, especially popular with the young; the opposite of the Café Norden. Popular meeting place and therefore always full. *Mon–Wed, 9 am–midnight, Thurs–Sat, 9 am–1 am, Sun, 10 am–midnight; Amagertorv 1*

## La Glace (96/B4)

★ ✿ Typical Danish cake shop, the oldest in Copenhagen and currently run by the fifth generation of the same family. Set in a house dating back to 1870, it is cosily furnished, but small and often full. Don't give up hope of finding a free table; it's worth popping in a second time. Speciality: the hot chocolate drink and the "sport cake". This was created in 1891 and is so complicated to make that the head pastry chef feels able to print the recipe and baking instructions in a commemorative booklet without fear of competition! The biscuits are an ideal souvenir, as well as a popular Christ-mas gift. *Mon–Fri, 8 am–6 pm, Sat, 9 am–5 pm, Sun, 11 am–5 pm; Skoubogade 3 (directly on the Strøget)*

## Hard Rock Café (96/A6)

♣ Copenhagen's current hot favourite among the younger clientele – locals and visitors alike – which can be said of most Hard Rock Cafés around the world. *Sun–Thurs, midday–midnight, Fri–Sat, midday–2 am; Vesterbrogade 3*

## Kransekagehuset (97/D4)

*Kransekage* is the name of the Danish ring-shaped cake with marzipan, just one of the specialities of the house, which comes closest to the traditional coffee house style.

*Mon–Thurs, 8 am–6 pm, Fri, 8 am–6.30 pm, Sat, 9 am–3 pm; Østergade 24B/at the corner of Pistolstræde*

## Café Norden (97/D4)

*Art nouveau* café, extending over two floors. Elegant surroundings, and fairly expensive, in spite of self-service. *Mon–Sat, 9 am–midnight, Sun, 10 am–midnight; Østergade 61*

## Pussy Galor's (104/A1)

Pussy Galor's Flying Circus, to give it its full name. Really trendy, from the design to the guests, everything is totally up-to-date. Like at the Sebastopol next door, a nice place to sit outside. *Mon–Fri, 8 am–2 am, Sat–Sun, 9 am–2 am; Skt. Hans Torv*

## Sabines Caféteria (96/B4)

⚡ Typical University-district café with mainly young customers. Nice place to sit and have a chat in, not as posh as other cafés maybe, but still agreeable. *Mon–Sat, 10 am–2 am, Sun, 2 pm–2 am; Teglgårdsstræde 4*

*The legendary beer is brewed behind this archway*

### Sebastopol (104/A1)

Pleasant café (with its own separate, posh brasserie) with plenty of tables out on the Skt. Hans Torv. *Sun–Wed, 9 am–1 am, Thurs–Sat, 9 am–2 am; Guldbergsgade 2*

### Café Sommersko (96/C4)

Very popular café in large, bright rooms on two floors. Recommended for its good breakfast and reasonably-priced small meals during the daytime. *Mon–Wed, 8 am–midnight, Thurs–Sat, 8 am–2 am, Sun, 9 am–midnight; Kronprinsensgade 6*

### Café Victor (97/D3–4)

❂ Cosy café, bar and restaurant (Danish and French cuisine) in the classical style. Elegant atmosphere; although it's a "see and be seen" establishment, the prices are reasonable. *Mon–Wed, 9 am–1 am, Thurs, 9 am–2 am, Fri–Sat, 9 am–4 am, Sun, 11 am–10 pm; Ny Østergade 8*

---
**PUB**
---

### Bryggeriet Apollo (96/A6)

Denmark's smallest brewery "Apollo", within the pub. Country-style cooking, washed down with a beer. Next to the Tivoli Gardens. *Mon–Wed, 11.30 am–midnight, Thurs–Sat, 11.30 am–2 am, Sun, 3 pm–midnight; Vesterbrogade 3*

---
**RESTAURANTS: CATEGORY 1**
---

*(Main course for one person, approximately 200–250 dkr)*

### L'Alsace (97/D4)

Restaurant specialising in the cuisine of the Alsace region of France. Idyllic setting in an inner courtyard. The view from the conservatory gives out onto half-timbered houses. *Mon–Sat, 11.30 am–mid-night; Ny Østergade 9/at the corner of Pistolstræde; Tel. 33 14 57 43*

### Balkonen (96/A–B6)

★ Superb view over the Tivoli Gardens from the first and second floors. Fine Danish and international dishes. *During the Tivoli season, daily midday–11.30 pm; Tivoli; Tel. 33 11 27 85*

### Blue Elephant (105/D5)

Located in the Radisson SAS Scandinavia Hotel, this restaurant offers original Thai cuisine in a genuine Thai setting. *Mon–Thurs, midday –2.30 pm, Sun–Wed, 6 pm–10.30 pm, Fri–Sat, 6 pm–11.30 pm; Amager Boulevard 70; Tel. 33 96 59 70*

### Den Gyldene Fortun (97/D5)

Seafood restaurant, serving freshly-caught fish daily. Pleasant setting on the canal. *Mon–Fri, midday–3 pm and 5 pm–10 pm, Sat–Sun, 6 pm–10 pm; Ved Stranden 18; Tel. 33 12 20 11*

### Den Sorte Ravn (97/E–F 4)

This is one of the most popular and most expensive Nyhavn restaurants, situated in an 18th-century house. Numerous businessmen among the diners, enjoying the French and Danish specialities. The tables stand directly on the side of the canal. *Daily 11.30 am–midnight; Nyhavn 14; Tel. 33 13 12 33*

### Divan 2 (96/B6)

Divan 2 was opened in the same year as the Tivoli Gardens, namely 1843. Magnificent view across the Tivoli Lake. Expensive interior decor is the setting for the best French cuisine in town. Excellent wine cellar. *During the Tivoli season, daily 11.30 am–11.30 pm; Tivoli; Tel. 33 12 51 51*

# Gourmet Restaurants in Copenhagen

## Era Ora (109/E4–5)

Bright, typically Italian in style, and the cuisine is unbeatable – the Era Ora is one of the best restaurants in town. *Mon–Sat, 6 pm–9 pm; Torvegade 62; Tel. 32 54 06 93*

## Kommandanten (101/D4)

The enchanting furnishings of this, the only two-star restaurant in Denmark is the work of florist and interior designer Tage Andersen, whose shop lies directly opposite. Traditional Danish cuisine, superb service. Don't forget to book a table! *Mon–Fri, midday–2 pm and 5.30 pm–10 pm, Sat, 5.30 pm–10 pm; Ny Adelgade 7; Tel. 33 12 09 90*

## Kong Hans Kælder (101/D4)

Daniel Letz, originally from Alsace, earned the first Michelin star in Scandinavia for this restaurant. It is located in a Gothic cellar which King Hans (1481–1513) used as a wine cellar. Very expensive restaurant, which also offers more reasonably-priced country-style cooking. *Mon–Sat, 6 pm–10 pm; Vingårdstræde 6; Tel. 33 11 68 68*

## Krogs Fiskerestaurant (100/C5)

One of the finest and most popular (and most expensive) fish restaurants in Copenhagen. Located in a house which dates back to the year 1798 and is most elegantly furnished. In fine weather, tables are set outside, so that diners can enjoy the view over the canal to the Church of Christiansborg Palace. *Mon–Sat, 11.30 am–4 pm and 5.30 pm–midnight; Gammel Strand 38; Tel. 33 15 89 15*

## Leonore Christine (101/E4)

Simply furnished, somewhat cramped but excellent restaurant in the oldest house at Nyhavn (1681). Discreet service, exquisite dishes and a tempting wine menu. *Daily midday–midnight; Nyhavn 9; Tel. 33 13 50 40*

## Nouvelle (100/C5)

First-class, very expensive restaurant (one Michelin star), offering Danish cuisine, the speciality of the house being fish. Excellent choice of wines. In the cellar is the more reasonably-priced lunchtime restaurant Lækerbisken which serves Danish specialities. *Mon–Fri, midday–4 pm and 5.30 pm–10 pm, Sat, 5.30 pm –10 pm; Gammel Strand 34; Tel. 33 13 50 18*

## Plaza (100/A6)

The hotel of the same name has recently been renovated and now includes an outstanding restaurant. Everything is just right: furnishings, atmosphere, service and, of course, the food, whether it be Italian, French, American or Danish. The menus are put together before the eyes of the guests. *Mon–Sat, 5.30 pm–10 pm; Bernstorffsgade 4; Tel. 33 14 15 19*

## Pakhuskælderen (97/E–F4)

Top-class Nyhavn restaurant, in a renovated storehouse (Hotel Nyhavn). Danish and French cuisine. *Mon–Sat, 6 pm–midnight; Nyhavn 71; Tel. 33 11 85 85*

## Sct. Gertruds Kloster (96/C3)

Dine by candlelight in this exclusive restaurant in a medieval convent cellar. The food is excellent and highly praised – and consequently expensive. Well-stocked wine cellar. *Daily 4 pm– 2 am; Hauser Plads 32; Tel. 33 14 66 30*

## RESTAURANTS: CATEGORY 2

*(Main course for one person, approximately 100–200 dkr)*

## els (97/E4)

★ The "Elk" can look back on a long tradition, beginning in the year 1853. Furnished with exquisite antiques, creating a welcoming atmosphere. The buffet and à la carte menu are excellent. *Mon–Sat, midday–3 pm and 5.30 pm–10 pm, Sun, 5.30 pm– 10 pm; Store Strandstræde 3; Tel. 33 14 13 41*

## Elverhøj (97/E–F4)

Refined restaurant located in a typical Nyhavn house from the 17th century. The speciality of the house is seafood. *Daily 11.30 am– 4 pm and 5.30 pm–10 pm; Nyhavn 23; Tel. 33 32 09 99*

## Færgekroen (96/A–B6)

A sea of flowers and the twittering of birds provide the background to the "Ferry Tankard" on the bank of the Tivoli Lake. Danish cooking, pleasant terrace and an entertainment programme from 8 pm. That's when it gets *hyggelig*, and the guests join in the singing. *During the Tivoli season, daily 10 am–10 pm; Tivoli; Tel. 33 12 94 12*

## Gråbrødretorv 21 (96/C4)

★ Small restaurant offering superb new Danish cuisine in old, country-style Danish surroundings. *Daily midday–midnight; Gråbrødretorv 21; Tel. 33 11 47 07*

## Ida Davidsen (97/E2–3)

★ ☉ The oldest *smørrebrød* restaurant in town, currently run by the fifth generation of the family. One hundred and fifty types of *smørrebrød*, large portions and mouth-watering creations. First-time visitors could be disappointed, since the restaurant rests very much on its 1970s laurels and could do with a lick of paint, not to mention the fact that it has become more expensive, too. *Mon–Fri, 10 am–5 pm, food served until 4 pm only; Store Kongensgade 70; Tel. 33 91 36 55*

## KGB (97/D–E3)

Noble restaurant, in shades of grey, blue and black – very much the place to be at the moment. Own vodka bar. Excellent menu, including non-Russian dishes. *Mon– Thurs, midday–midnight; Fri, midday– 2 am, Sat, 10 am–2 am; Dronningens Tværgade 22; Tel. 33 36 07 70*

## Slotskælderen hos Gitte Kik (104/C3)

★ For the locals is the "Gitte Kik" the better of the two most famous Copenhagen smørrebrød restaurants. Situated in a central position, close to Castle Island, it attracts many diplomats and members of parliament. Conservative surroundings, but with a superb choice of smørrebrød delicacies. *Tues–Sat,*

*Tivoli's culinary delights are second to none. There's no end of garden cafés and restaurants to choose from*

10 am–5 pm, food served until 4 pm only; Fortunstræde 4; Tel. 33 11 15 37

## Parnas (97/D4)

This is 100 per cent Denmark: the food, the atmosphere and the setting, everything is the way the Danes love it. In the evenings there's music and dancing until late at night. *Mon–Thurs, 5 pm–3 am, Fri–Sat, 5 pm–5 am; Lille Kongensgade 16; Tel. 33 11 49 10*

## Peder Oxe (96/C4)

★ Large dining rooms, light, well-scrubbed floors plus a welcoming, yet elegant atmosphere – only the Danes can achieve precisely this mixture. Below the restaurant in the Romanesque cellar is a wine bar, which is admittedly very full at weekends. *Daily 11.30 am–1 am; Gråbrødretorv 11; Tel. 33 11 00 77*

## Skipperkroen (97/E4)

★ The name "Sailor's Tankard" is misleading; this restaurant, café and bar is more up-market than you'd imagine. Located in two neighbouring Nyhavn houses, linked by a covered area rather like a conservatory. There are also tables on the banks of the canal. Good food, good wine menu and particularly friendly staff. *Daily midday–5 pm and 5.30–midnight; Nyhavn 27; Tel. 33 11 99 06*

## Teaterkælderen (104/A4)

Pleasant restaurant with good food, though it is better suited to large parties than individual diners. The "Theatre Cellar" is aptly named, since the staff – all drama students – regale you with arias from the world of opera and operetta while serving the meals! *Tues–Sat, 5 pm–1 am, Sun, 5 pm–midnight; Gammel Kongevej 29; Tel. 33 25 75 00*

## Valhal (96/A–B6)

Step into the world of the Nordic sagas in this Tivoli restaurant. *During the Tivoli season, daily midday–11 pm; Tivoli; Tel. 33 14 67 40*

## RESTAURANTS: CATEGORY 3

*(Main course for one person, less than 100 dkr)*

### India Palace (96/B6)

Do you like Indian food? Indian restaurant with typical Indian buffet and à la carte menu, at reasonable prices. *Daily 11 am –midnight; H. C. Andersens Boulevard 13; Tel. 33 91 04 08*

### Kronborg (96/C5)

Welcoming restaurant with wooden-beam ceiling and open fire. At lunchtime there is a reasonably-priced *smørrebrød* selection and other dishes. *Mon–Sat, 11 am–6 pm; Brolæggerstræde 12; Tel. 33 13 07 08*

### Spiseloppen (105/E4)

✪ Simple, vegetarian restaurant in in the borough Christiania. *Tues–Sun, 5 pm–11 pm; Bådmandsstræde 32; Tel. 31 57 95 58*

## WINE BARS

### Frimands Quarteer (96/C4)

Dimly-lit, cosy wine bar, furnished in rustic style. Atmosphere to match. Also serves food. *Daily 11 am–1 am; Gråbrødretorv; Tel. 33 12 96 86*

### Hviids Vinstue (97/D4)

★ ✪ Copenhagen's oldest wine bar has been in business since 1723. Cramped, cosy, dark and smoke-filled – what better way to get chatting to the locals. No food, but all manner of liquid refreshment. At Christmas this is the best place to try *Jule-Gløg. Sun–Thurs, 10 am–1 am, Fri–Sat, 10 am–2 am; May–Sept: closed on Sundays; Kongens Nytorv 19; Tel. 33 15 10 64*

---

### Smørrebrød: more than just your average sandwich

In 1888 Oscar Davidsen – great-grandfather of Ida Davidsen, who gave her name to the most famous smørrebrød restaurant in Copenhagen – had a brilliant idea. Your average customer can drink more *øl* and *akvavit* on a full stomach, he thought. So he decided to start serving food in his pub on the Store Kongensgade. Since the kitchen was minute, to say the least, he couldn't manage much more than a sandwich – the *smørrebrød* was born! It's made with bread and it's got butter on it, but the *smørrebrød* is a far cry from your common or garden sandwich. A Danish *smørrebrød* is a way of life which testifies to the Danes' creativity and is as good as a proper meal at the best of times. Tourists who, in their ignorance, order half a dozen "sandwiches" in one go, to be sure of conquering their hunger, are confronted with an insurmountable task. Normally, two or three of these creations are sufficient to see you through from *frokost* in the morning to *middag* in the evening. All kinds of seafood finds its way onto a *smørrebrød*: eels, salmon, plaice, crab, prawns and caviar, plus cooked meats, ham, cheese and eggs – in the most amazing combinations. You can't go wrong with a *smørrebrød* – but only at lunchtime. In the eyes of the experts, to order a *smørrebrød* in the evening is a classic *faux pas*. On the other hand, though, it's ok to eat your *smørrebrød* with a knife and fork.

# Shopping with style

*A flower shop like a museum, hand made sweets, mini paper theatres - Copenhagen's retail landscape has more to offer than just Danish design*

The advertising slogan which claims that shopping in Copenhagen is addictive is no exaggeration. Danish design is at the top of visitors' shopping lists when they come here, whether it be works of art, everyday items, furniture or fashion articles. Finding a souvenir is never a problem. Popular choices are items of glassware, clothing made of wool in the typical Danish style – clear, bold colours, casual cuts, not too tight – plus wooden toys. Kay Bojesen has created a number of best-sellers in this field, such as elephants, monkeys and even Royal Life Guards!

Shopping is made easy for the visitor to Copenhagen; the most interesting shops are situated in the pedestrian zone ★ Strøget or in its numerous side streets, for example around the University or in the Læderstræde and Kompagnistræde, which are also pedestrian-only.

Of course, it is also possible to shop outside the confines of the old town. Gammel Kongevej in *Frederiksberg* is, for example, a popular though busy and noisy shopping street. A good range of shops can also be found at the airport, where many famous names have set up smaller branches of their bigger shops in town. Experience shows, however, that sooner or later most visitors end up in the old town again, with its small boutiques, large department stores and specialist shops, many of which bear the title "Purveyor to the Royal Court" – a distinction which is bestowed only once within each retail branch.

In 1985 a number of leading Danish companies specialising in arts and crafts joined together under the brand name "Royal Copenhagen": the Royal Porcelain Factory, Royal Copenhagen, porcelain manufacturer Bing & Grøndahl, silversmith's Georg Jensen and Holmegaard Glass, plus Illums Bolighus, specialists in modern design. Each of the companies in the Royal Copenhagen Group has a sales outlet on the Amagertorv (and others, for example at the airport).

The laws governing trading hours have recently been relaxed, to allow shops to open between 6 am and 6 pm, though

*Shop till you drop on the Strøget: it's addictive! Illum has four storeys under the glass dome*

little use is made of this opportunity. In general, shops open at 9.30 am or 10 am and close at 6 pm (occasionally 7 or 8 pm). On Saturdays they close at 1 pm, department stores at 2 pm. On the first Saturday in the month shops may stay open from 9 am until 5 pm, in June, July and August this applies to every Saturday.

## ANTIQUES

Twenty antique dealers and junk shops are to be found in Nørrebro, chiefly on the ★ Ravnsborgade and in the streets round about. In fine weather in particular, the area resembles a giant flea market.

A further mecca for antiques fans is the area around the Læderstræde, Kompagnistræde and Farvergade in the old town, as well as Bredgade, with its array of antique shops, auction rooms and galleries. The department store Illum on the Strøget has its own antiques department on the third floor. Further dealers are scattered over the entire old part of town.

**Bastard** (104/C3)
Furniture, porcelain and glass from the 1970s – including some very attractive items – are sold in this basement shop. *Læderstræde 36*

# MARCO POLO SELECTION: SHOPPING

**1 Strøget**
One of the most famous shopping streets in the world – and rightly so (page 57)

**2 Tage Andersen**
He transformed a simple flower shop into a museum (page 59)

**3 Sømods Bolcher**
One hundred years of hand-made sweets (page 59)

**4 Illum**
Copenhagen's luxury department store even has its own antiques department (page 62)

**5 Priors Dukketeatre**
Paper theatres and cut-out sheets in a basement shop (page 63)

**6 Georg Jensen**
Silver in the tradition of the famous silversmith (page 64)

**7 Royal Copenhagen**
Royal Porcelain Factory with guided tours for interested visitors (page 63)

**8 Ravnsborgade**
Antique dealers in abundance – 20 of them, in fact. On sunny days, it's like a giant, top-notch flea market (page 58)

**9 Illums Bolighus**
Danish design for the home and for every pocket (page 61)

**10 W. Ø. Larsen**
Hand-made pipes in the showroom and Tobacco Museum (page 63)

## Royal Copenhagen Antiques (96/C4)

Stylish shop, selling only antiques produced by those manufacturers who are part of the Royal Copenhagen Group: porcelain from Royal Copenhagen and Bing & Grøndahl, silver from Georg Jensen and old Holmegaard glass. In the same building you will also find the tiny *Georg Jensen Museum*, which has a display of silverware made between 1904 and 1940 in the famous master craftsman's workshop and also personal mementoes (open during usual trading hours). *Amagertorv 6*

### AUCTIONEERS

## Bruun Rasmussen Kunstauktioner (97/E3)

Largest auction rooms in the city which stages international auctions in the fields of art and antiques and also hosts smaller sales of, for example, wines, firearms and books. *Bredgade 33*

### AMBER

## Rav Specialisten

The only "specialist amber dealer" in Copenhagen, as he calls himself, has three shops; one is situated in the Cruise Information Centre at Langelinien (**101/E5**), one on the Strøget (which has recently moved to a new address: Frederiksberggade 35, **96/B5**) and a large shop, Ravhuset, directly on Nyhavn, at the corner of Store Strandgæde (**97/E4**). Here you will also find a small *Amber Museum* which tells the story of amber in the Baltic region. *Mon-Thurs, 10 am-6 pm,*

*Fri, 10 am-7 pm, Sat-Sun, 10 am-6pm; admission: adults: 20, children: 10 dkr; Kongens Nytorv 2; Tel. 33 11 88 03*

### FLOWERS

## Tage Andersen (97/D4)

★ His shop is much more than just a simple flower shop: Tage Andersen's fanciful creations made of wrought iron are no longer mere representations of flowers. They have become exclusive decorative items in their own right, which transform the shop – with its glass pavilion containing exotic plants in a half-timbered rear courtyard – into a charming little museum. Tage Andersen regards his shop as such, and charges those people who come to look around rather than to buy an admission fee of 40 dkr. A magnificent coffee-table book showing the artist's works (with commentaries in Danish and English) is available in the shop for 800 dkr. *Ny Adelgade 12*

## Erik Bering (96/C4)

Supplier of flowers to the Royal Court, with an attractive window display through which you get a glimpse of the small shop behind. *Købmagergade 7*

### CONFECTIONERY

## Sømods Bolcher (96/B4)

★ You can smell the old sweets factory, which is located in a rear courtyard, a mile off – but it's a pleasant smell, since Sømods Bolcher, Purveyors to the Royal Court, use only natural flavourings in their products. Here, the sweets are still made

*Inspired Danish glass design, enticingly displayed at Bolighus*

by hand, as they were a hundred years ago, when the little company was founded. Sømods Bolcher is probably the only manufacturer of confectionery in the world which upholds this tradition. It is possible not only to watch the sweet-makers at work, but also to buy the end products, in all shapes and sizes, colours and patterns, among them the Danish flag! It never ceases to amaze visitors how the shop assistant in the antiquated shop manages to distinguish between all the unlabelled sweet tins. They even make sweets for diabetics, too. Visitors may watch production as follows: *Mon-Fri, 9.15 am-3.15 pm; admission: free; Nørregade 36;* in a second shop next door, *Nørregade 34,* you can also find out how sweets are made: *Mon-Fri, 10.30 am-4.15 pm*

## BOOKS

### Paludan (96/A-B5)

Paludan – this means heaven on earth for bookworms! Here, in this old-established and well-known bookseller's with its own second-hand book department, you can browse to your heart's content. *Fiolstræde*

## DUVETS

### Ofelia (96/C4)

A surprising number of visiting businessmen and -women from abroad take home feather duvets as a souvenir of their trip to Copenhagen. Consequently, this world-famous specialist dealer, Ofelia, which has an unbelievably wide range of products, sells its duvets in a handy carrier bag. *Amagertorv 3*

## DESIGN

### Artium (96/A6)

A little on the pompous side, perhaps, the shop in the Rathausarkaden likes to call itself "Scandinavian Design Centre". Nevertheless, the selection of tasteful gift ideas is good. *H. C. Andersens Boulevard/at the corner of Vesterbrogade*

### Bang & Olufsen (97/D4)

The completely redesigned and modernised Bang & Olufsen Centre presents the complete product range of this hi-fi manufacturer who has set new standards world-wide in terms of design in the electronics industry. *Østergade 3-5*

### Illums Bolighus (96/C4)

★ The furniture store (*bolig* means "home"), which has no connection with the department store of the same name, has four floors full of tasteful items for the home; eye-catching glass and tableware, carpets and textiles, fashion and furniture. The whole spectrum of Scandinavian – and above all Danish – design is on display here. *Amagertorv 10 (There is now a branch in the Vesterbrogade between the Hard Rock Café and the Tivoli ticket office called Illums Bolighus Tivoli.)*

## FLEA MARKETS

### Frederiksberg (102–103/C–D3)

The flea market where anyone can sell things is located on the car park in Smallegade, directly behind the Town Hall in Frederiksberg. *May-Nov.: Sat, 10 am-2 pm*

### Gammel Strand (104/C3)

Relatively expensive and classy flea market in the most attractive setting imaginable: the stalls line the canal banks, the street cafés tempt you to take a well-earned break from browsing. *May-Sept: Sat, 10 am-2 pm*

### Israels Plads (96/B3)

Expensive antiques flea market behind the Nørreport railway station and the fruit and vegetable market. *May-Oct.: Sat, 8 am-2 pm*

### Nørrebros Runddel (99/E6)

Flea market at the northern end of the Assistens Kirkegård, specialising in art and craft objects. Many stall holders present their own works for sale. *May-Oct.: Sat, 10 am-2 pm*

## GLASS

### Hinz/Kjær Design (97/D4)

The modern Danish glassworks, whose workshops are in Gilleleje on the northernmost tip of Zealand, has a sales outlet in Copenhagen. The attractive products on sale here, whether from series production or individual items, (drinking glasses, bowls, vases) testify to the high standard of glass-blowing which has been achieved in Denmark today. Let yourself be tempted to take a day-trip to Gilleleje, where you can watch the glass-blowers at work: *Fri, 11 am-5 pm and Sat, 10 am-2 pm; Østergade 24C/at the corner of Pistolstræde*

### Royal Copenhagen Crystal (96/C4)

Danish and international household glass and decorative items produced in series or as individual pieces are on sale in an old town house on the Amagertorv. Centrepiece of the shop, which belongs to the Royal Copenhagen Group, are items of Holmegaard glass. The glassworks, in operation since 1825, lies in Næstved in South Zealand, approximately 80 km from Copenhagen, and is open to visitors. *To book a visit, Tel. 55 54 62 00; Amagertorv 8*

### Nyhavns Glaspusterie (105/E4)
Typical Danish glass-blower's workshop, such as you'll find in many holiday regions. Visitors may look over the shoulder of the craftsmen as they work. The small gallery which belongs to the workshop has a display of beautiful series-produced glasses and also individual items of high artistic value – expensive, but very tasteful souvenirs! *June-Sept.: Tues-Sun, 10 am-6 pm; Oct.-May: Tues-Sat, midday-6 pm; Toldbodgade 4; www.glasshouse.dk*

### CHEESE

### J. Ch. Andersens Czar (96/C4)
J. Christian Andersen's descendants run this delicatessen, selling fruit, salads and cheese, cheese, cheese! The wide range of varieties on offer show there's more to Danish cheese than Danish Blue. *Købmagergade 32*

### DEPARTMENT STORES

### Illum (97/D4)
★ The finest shopping emporium in town with, as you would expect from such an establishment, the usual range of international goods. The sales rooms extend over four floors,

underneath a beautiful glass dome. They also offer a wide selection of international newspapers and magazines. From the Købmagergade you can take the glass-walled lift straight up to the busy restaurant and café on the fourth floor. *Østergade 52*

### Magasin du Nord (97/D4)
The ultimate department store – Scandinavia's largest – belongs to the Magasin chain, which has long since taken over its arch rival Illum. The range of goods on offer is on a par with comparable stores of this size. The magnificent façade is a remnant of the former "Hotel du grand Nord", which was erected here well over a hundred years ago and which was converted into a huge department store in 1893. The building was renovated to mark its hundredth birthday. *Kongens Nytorv*

### FASHION

Fashion is certainly not the main reason why people come to Copenhagen, although you'll find everything here which you would expect from an international capital. The same can be said of the many boutiques, especially those in the old town, although hardly any of them are particularly striking. Here are a few examples.

### Red/Green (97/D4)
Chic and expensive, for him and her. *Bremerholm 1*

Some shops commission fashion designers to put together their own in-house collections, which they sell at reasonably acceptable prices.

## Noa Noa (96/B5)

Colourful collection for women only, between the ages of 15 and 50 (and older) here in the boutique of owner/designer Harald Helstein. *Larsbjørnstræde 16*

As far as footwear is concerned, the situation is pretty much the same. The shoes on offer in Copenhagen are nothing to write home about. Consequently we can only recommend one shop.

## Bruno & Joel (97/E4)

Simple, but good quality and therefore expensive: these are the words which best describe the shoes you'll find at Bruno & Joel. Originally specialising in designer shoes for both men and women, they now only cater for women. They do have a large selection of top-quality Italian and French styles, though. *Store Strandstræde 9*

### MUSEUM JEWELLERY

## Museums Kopi Smykker (97/D4)

Here you will find hand-made jewellery made of gold, silver, gold-plated bronze and bronze. These are replicas of Scandinavian jewellery from the early Bronze Age and the Viking era. *Grønnegade 6.* In addition to the obligatory branch in the transit area of the airport, there is also a shop on the Strøget, at *Frederiksberggade 2.*

### PAPER THEATRE

## Priors Dukketeatre (96/C4)

★ Originally, Hanne Nelander's more than one-hundred-year-old shop stood in Købmagergade 52; now she has moved to basement premises in Ole Suhrs Gade. She has parted company with her paper theatre museum, a wonderful collection of model theatres made entirely of paper. This is now owned by the folk theatre. In her new shop she still sells paper cut-out sheets of model theatres and a range of theatre scripts to go with them. As ever, Hanne Nelander writes plays, together with friends, especially for these miniature works of art. The Priors Dukketeatre also has a selection of re-prints of fine, old cut-out sheets. *Thurs-Fri, midday-6 pm, Sat, 10 am-2 pm; Ole Suhrs Gade 13*

### PIPES

## W. Ø. Larsen (96/C4)

★ The pipe-smoker's every whim is catered for here. This distinguished shop specialises in valuable, hand-made pipes and is, of course, one of that noteworthy group of retailers who supply the Royal Court. Larsen's also includes a small *Tobacco Museum* next door, with pipes from all over the world, tobacco tins and other pipe-smoker's paraphernalia. Admission is free. *Amagertorv 9*

### PORCELAIN

## Rosenthal (96/B5)

The Rosenthal studio has a selection of international porcelain designs for sale, plus pieces by Danish craftsmen such as Bjørn Wiinblad. (Also on sale is a range of fine glass items.) *Frederiksberggade 21*

## Royal Copenhagen (96/C4)

★ The "Flora Danica" service is the most famous set of tableware ever produced by the porcelain factory which was founded in 1775, and it is still being manufactured today. For the slightly smaller purse, there is the equally popular flower-print design, "Mussel-malet". The collection is not limited to old, traditional designs, but also features the work of modern artists and craftsmen. Visitors can take part in a one-hour guided tour of the Royal Porcelain Factory in Frederiksberg, during which they can follow the various stages of production at first hand. In addition to the production site in Frederiksberg (**102/C3**), Royal Copenhagen also has attractive sales rooms in the most beautiful house on the Amagertorv. Here, from May to September, during normal trading hours, shoppers can take a peek over the shoulder of a porcelain painter at work. *Guided tours in English: Mon-Fri, 9 am, 10 am, 11 am, 1 pm and 2 pm; admission: adults: 25 dkr, children: free; Smallegade 47; bus: 1, 14, 39. Sales rooms: Amagertorv 6*

## PULLOVERS

### Sweater Market            (96/B5)
In Europe's largest sweater shop - if you believe the advertising claim - you could find that you can't see the wood for the trees, so to speak. Two floors are packed full of typical Nordic sweater designs - in every conceivable colour, size and pattern. The staff will let you browse for hours on end, without trying to force you into buying something. Prices, too, are surprisingly reasonable. *Frederiksberggade 15*

## ODDS & ENDS

### Søstrene Grenes          (96/C4)
If you're a fan of useless odds and ends and knick-knacks from all over the world, then this is the place for you. This tiny shop is always busy and is a treasure-trove

for those who are on the look-out for a cheap and cheerful present. The cheapest items on offer cost as little as 13 Øre. *Amagertorv 29*

## SILVER

### Georg Jensen            (96/C4)
★ According to many people, Georg Jensen (1866-1935) was the greatest silversmith of the past three centuries. He began working with silver in 1904, and the business which he founded and which bears his name continues the tradition to this day. It now belongs to the Royal Copenhagen Group. His jewellery designs from the 1930s are being produced again and are very popular with customers. The company also employs a large number of young silversmiths and designers who produce items reflecting their own personal styles and talents. Each considers it a privilege to work in his profession. From May to September you can watch one of the silversmiths at work in the Georg Jensen shop on the Amagertorv (there are other branches, e.g. at the airport). *Amagertorv 4*

### Peter Krog              (97/E3)
This silver dealer is a specialist for second-hand Georg Jensen creations. *Bredgade 4*

## WINE

### Kjær & Sommerfeldt       (97/D3)
In recent years, the selection of wines available on the Danish market has improved dramatically, and prices are generally on the decline. You would be hard put, however, to find a better selection than here, both in terms of quality

and scope. This exquisite wine dealer also features special offers and occasional sales, so that even the finest labels come within reach of the average customer. *Gammel Mønt 4*

## FURNISHINGS

### Lysberg, Hansen & Therp (97/E3)
Furniture and decorative items for the home - not necessarily the ideal souvenir, but plenty of ideas to take with you. *Bredgade 3*

## PEWTER

### Tin Centret (97/D4)
This shop claims to have the largest selection of pewter in the whole of Scandinavia, and they are not exaggerating. The range is incredible. Fans and collectors of all things pewter will be well catered for here. *Ny Østergade 2*

*Porcelain from Copenhagen is a favourite souvenir*

# A good night's sleep

*Hotels don't have to have five stars to be luxurious and elegant.
If you're looking for something out of the ordinary,
why not try a former warehouse?*

As is the case with restaurants in Copenhagen, the hotels here are generally of a medium to high standard; genuine luxury hotels are rare and so-called dream hotels are non-existent. In the whole of Denmark there is not a single hotel which, by international standards, is worthy of five stars, not even the Hotel *D'Angleterre* and the *SAS Scandinavia Hotel*. In and around Copenhagen, there are approximately one hundred hotels with a total of 18,000 beds.

Twenty hotels at least offer parking facilities in their own garages - a blessing in a city where parking spaces are rare, due to the fact that the inner city is divided into restricted-parking zones.

In the summer of 1997 an official hotel classification system was introduced in Denmark. Hotels participate in the inspections on a voluntary basis, which means that some hotels do not qualify for a star rating (which does not necessarily mean they are any worse than the ones that do). In Copenhagen especially, the classification process has produced an interesting side-effect: there are now considerably more hotel restaurants than there used to be, since in order to achieve a rating of three stars, a hotel must have a restaurant. Copenhagen's hotels are not cheap, even the more modest establishments charge around 600 dkr for a single room with private bath. Double rooms with private bath are not much more expensive; they start at approximately 900 dkr. In the more expensive hotels, the price for a single room can reach 1,700 dkr, a double room then costs 1,900 dkr (in some cases, the sky's the limit!).

One night in a Youth Hostel (the Danish variety are mostly of hotel standard) or in a young people's hotels can be had for as little as 60 dkr, going up to a maximum of 135 dkr, plus the cost of breakfast. In some cases, it is possible to cook a light meal yourself.

Hotel rooms in Copenhagen can be booked in advance in writing at the following address: *Hotelbooking København, Gammel Kongevej 1, DK-1610 København V. You can of course also book by fax (0045/33 25 74 10) or by telephone (0045/33 25 38 44, Mon–Thurs, 9 am–4 pm, Fri 9 am-3 pm). The following agency also takes hotel bookings: Easy-Book, Århusgade 33-35, DK-2100 København Ø; Fax*

*D'Angleterre: the best hotel in town has retained all its charm*

*0045/35 38 06 37. You can also call 0045/35 38 00 37; (all year round: Mon-Fri, 9 am-6 pm, Sat, 9 am-2 pm).*

Can you take the risk of coming to Copenhagen without booking your accommodation in advance? The answer depends greatly on the time of year you want to travel and the calendar of events scheduled for that period. At least the accommodation service of the hotel booking department is well organised (Copenhagen Tourist Office). *Opening times: Jan.–April and mid-Sept.–Dec: Mon-Fri, 9 am-4.30 pm, Sat, 9 am-1.30 pm; May–mid-Sept: daily 9 am–9 pm*

You can save a lot of money on accommodation by booking a package deal. Many travel companies include Copenhagen in their programme and offer holidays in the city, allowing you to choose how you get there.

## HOTELS: CATEGORY 1

*(De luxe: from 1,200 dkr per double room)*

### D'Angleterre (97/D4)

★ Anybody who's anybody – or just thinks they are – has to stay here. It is, quite simply, as far as image is concerned, the best and the oldest hotel in the city. Its location alone, on the Kongens Nytorv, is magnificent. *130 rooms; Kongens Nytorv 34; Tel. 3312 00 95; Fax 33 12 11 18; e-mail: sales@remmen.dk*

### Kong Frederik (96/A5)

Very good, welcoming hotel, furnished in traditional, classical style, but with every modern conve-

## MARCO POLO SELECTION: HOTELS

**1 D'Angleterre**
The oldest hotel just happens to be the best (page 68)

**2 Plaza Hotel**
The Library Bar, with its whiff of Empire, is worth every penny of the stiff hotel bill (page 69)

**3 Radisson SAS Scandinavia Hotel**
Caters to your every whim. It's even got a casino – the only one in town (page 69)

**4 Admiral**
Luxury in the converted storehouse – including the view over the harbour (page 69)

**5 Nyhavn Hotel**
Yet another former storehouse, this time with a romantic note (page 69)

**6 Radisson SAS Globetrotter**
Comfortable and well-equipped hotel, handy for the airport (page 70)

**7 Savoy Hotel**
The guests all agree, value for money is guaranteed here (page 71)

**8 Selandia**
This hotel is known for its particularly friendly service (page 71)

nience. *110 rooms; Vester Voldgade 25; Tel. 33 12 59 02; Fax 33 93 59 01; e-mail: sales@remmen.dk*

## Phoenix (97/E3)

The somewhat uninspiring exterior is deceptive; this is an excellent hotel with a high standard of comfort. *212 rooms; Bredgade 37; Tel. 33 95 95 00; Fax 33 33 98 33; e-mail: PhoenixCopenhagen@arp-hansen.dk*

## Radisson SAS Royal Hotel (96/A6)

This hotel, too, offers more facilities than most others in Copenhagen, for example a fitness centre and sauna. Situated right in the centre of town, it may not look very special from the outside, but its modern, typically Danish design is impressive. Architect and interior designer Arne Jacobsen was responsible for the interior decoration, and was called in to take charge of the recent redesigning of the hotel. *266 rooms; Hammerichsgade 1; Tel. 33 14 14 12; Fax 33 14 14 21*

## Radisson SAS Scandinavia Hotel (105/D5)

★ Although this hotel is very large, it still manages to seem luxurious and stylish. It offers a wide range of amenities, including a bar, casino, indoor swimming pool and health and fitness centre. *542 rooms; Amager Boulevard 70; Tel. 33 11 23 24; Fax 31 57 01 93*

## Scandic Hotel Copenhagen (104/A4)

⤷ Large, but equally luxurious hotel of international calibre. What's more, it affords the visitor a fabulous view across the Skt. Jørgens lake. *471 rooms; Vester Søgade 6; Tel. 33 14 35 35; Fax 33 32 12 23*

## Plaza (96/A6)

★ The Library Bar of the hotel is famous, and rightly so, for its amazingly cosy and welcoming atmosphere. Now that the public rooms have been renovated, including the excellent restaurant, it's the turn of the guest rooms to gradually receive an overhaul. Eventually, the entire hotel, built in 1913 close to the station, will have been returned to its former glory. *93 rooms; Bernstorffsgade 4; Tel. 33 14 92 62; Fax 33 93 93 62*

## HOTELS: CATEGORY 2

*(Mid-range: from 950 dkr per double room)*

## Admiral (104/B4)

★ This big hotel is located in a long, two-hundred-year-old former storehouse. It is comfortable, offers excellent service and stands directly on the harbour, close to the Amalienborg Palace. *366 rooms; Tolbodgade 24-28; Tel. 33 11 82 82; Fax 33 32 55 42; e-mail: admiral@admiralhotel.dk*

## Neptun (97/E–F3)

This tasteful, small hotel can look back on one hundred years of service. It is ideally placed for visits to the harbour, theatre and the business quarter. Pleasant restaurant serving good Danish cuisine. *15 suites, 136 rooms; Skt. Annæ Plads 14-20; Tel. 33 13 89 00; Fax 33 14 12 50; e-mail: info@neptun-group.dk*

## Nyhavn Hotel (97/F4)

★ ⤷ The building was originally one of the old harbour warehouses. Now turned into a superb hotel, it offers a wonderful view over the Nyhavn canal. The added designation "romantic"

*Admiral Hotel: stay the night in an old storehouse directly on the harbour*

is well-earned, though the rooms are a little on the small side. *82 rooms; Nyhavn 71; Tel. 33 11 85 85; Fax 33 93 15 85*

### Opera (97/E4)
Cosy hotel in first-rate location on the Kongens Nytorv. English-style restaurant and bar. Following renovation work, the hotel provides excellent quality throughout. *87 rooms; Tordenskjoldsgade 15; Tel. 33 12 15 19; Fax 33 32 12 82*

### Palace Hotel (96/B5)
Refined hotel with very pleasant rooms, situated directly on the Town Hall Square. *162 rooms; Rådhuspladsen 57; Tel. 33 14 40 50; Fax 33 14 52 79; e-mail: anders.emborg @principalhotels.co.uk*

### Radisson SAS Globetrotter Hotel (U/E6)
★ Modern, comfortable hotel located close to the airport, featur-

ing its own indoor swimming pool and fitness club. *197 rooms; Engvej 171; Tel. 32 87 02 02; Fax 32 87 02 20*

### Sophie Amalie (97/F4)
From the outside, this hotel does not look very promising, but once inside, the friendly atmosphere and standard of comfort more than make up for this. Danish-style furnishings and design. Situated between Amalienborg and Nyhavn and thus the ideal position for Copenhagen visitors. *134 rooms; Skt. Annæ Plads 21; Tel. 33 13 34 00; Fax 33 11 77 07*

### CPH Triton (104/A4–5)
The hotel dates back to the turn of the last century and was carefully renovated some years ago. The 123 rooms are furnished in typical Danish style. *Helgolandsgade 7-11; Tel. 33 31 32 66; Fax 33 31 69 70*

## HOTELS: CATEGORY 3

*(Basic: from 600 dkr per double room)*

### Absalon Hotel          (104/A4–5)
Large hotel in central location, close to the station. It has a certain charm, and sets great store by personal service. *253 rooms; Helgolandsgade 15; Tel. 33 24 22 11; Fax 33 24 34 11; e-mail: info@absalon-hotel.dk*

### Missions Hotellet Ansgar (104/A4)
Simple, reasonably-priced hotel in good position. Mission hotels have a long tradition in Denmark and are run no differently than other modest establishments. *87 rooms; Colbjørnsensgade 29; Tel. 33 21 21 96; Fax 33 21 61 91*

### Astoria          (96/A6)
Built in 1935 and lovingly renovated and modernised, the hotel is known for its good service. Close to the main railway station. *94 rooms; Banegårdspladsen 4; Tel. 33 14 14 19; Fax 33 14 08 02*

### Esplanaden          (97/E2–3)
Medium-sized, reasonable hotel, which has been completely renovated. *116 rooms; Bredgade 78; Tel. 33 91 32 00; Fax 33 91 32 39; e-mail: copenhagen.amager@danhostel.dk*

### Hebron          (104/A4)
Quiet family-run hotel situated close to the main railway station. Built in 1900, but with all modern amenities. *110 rooms; Helgolandsgade 4; Tel. 33 31 69 06; Fax 33 31 90 67*

### Savoy Hotel          (96/A6)
★ This is no plush hotel, as the name and the *Art Deco* façade would suggest, but a tourist class hotel where value for money is guaranteed. The reception area has been moved from the rear courtyard to the front, looking out onto the Vesterbrogade. *69 rooms; Vesterbrogade 34; Tel. 33 31 40 73; Fax 33 26 75 01*

### Selandia          (104/A4)
★ Relatively small, completely renovated hotel in a central location. Known among frequent Copenhagen visitors for its friendly and personal service. *84 rooms; Helgolandsgade 12; Tel. 33 31 46 10; Fax 33 31 46 10*

## FOR YOUNG PEOPLE

### Copenhagen Danhotel Bellahøj          (U/D5)
Youth Hostel situated in the parish of Brønshøj, 6 km from the centre of Copenhagen. *250 beds, 39 family rooms; Herbergvejen 8, Brønshøj; Tel. 38 28 97 15*

### Danhotel Amager          (U/E5)
Reasonably-priced, very large Youth Hostel, approximately 4 km from the city centre. *528 beds, 144 rooms, all suitable for accommodating families; Vejlands Allé 200; Tel. 32 52 29 08; e-mail: copenhagen.amager @danhostel.dk*

A cheap alternative (overnight stay, without breakfast, for two people: *585 dkr*) is available at both of the new Cab Inns in Frederiksberg, modest hotels with four-bed rooms:

### Cab Inn Copenhagen          (103/E–F3)
*86 rooms; Danasvej 32-2; Tel. 33 21 04 00; Fax 33 21 74 09*

### Cab Inn Scandinavia          (103/F3–4)
*201 rooms; Vodroffsvej 57; Tel. 35 36 11 11; Fax 35 36 11 14*

# Copenhagen diary

*Copenhagen never was one for showing off –*
*many celebrations take place on the quiet*

It must be said that Copenhagen has never earned – or claimed – a reputation as a great festival city. Even the year 1996, when the Danish capital was chosen as the 12th European City of Culture, did little to change matters, despite the fact that a number of interesting and much acclaimed events were staged in celebration. You would be hard put to find a tourist who had packed his bags in order to come to the city on the Øresund just for one particular cultural highlight – with the possible exception of more discerning jazz fans. Copenhagen's festivals and celebrations are perhaps a little more self-effacing, taking place "on the quiet", so to speak. Which is not to say that the city offers little which could compete on an international level. On the contrary, the Ballet Festival in Frederiksberg and, of course, the Copenhagen Jazz Festival are prime examples. What is perhaps more important for the Copenhageners than drawing comparisons

*What would Copenhagen be without the Changing of the Guard? The replacement guard marches over from Rosenborg Palace*

with other countries, is the ability to really celebrate and enjoy each event on its own merits – and they certainly know how to do that! Their enthusiasm for all cultural events, whether local or national, is infectious. Each performance is savoured like a good meal or an interesting conversation.

## DAILY EVENTS

### Changing of the Guard

★Everyday, at noon, the ceremony of the Changing of the Guard is performed on the Castle Square at the Amalienborg Palace. Prior to this, the Royal Life Guards march, in their blue (or red ceremonial) uniforms, from their barracks at the Rosenborg Palace through the city to the royal residence. From Easter to the end of November, when the Queen is in residence at Fredensborg Palace, the procession and ceremony are performed without musical accompaniment. Otherwise, the guards are accompanied by a band consisting of non-military musicians. In winter, when the Changing of the Guard is performed with all the trimmings, you had better find a good place to stand as soon as possible.

# MARCO POLO SELECTION: EVENTS & FESTIVALS

**1 Changing of the Guard**
A treat not only for fans of the monarchy (page 73)

**2 Carnival**
Whitsun with a difference: the rhythm of the samba in the cool North (page 75)

**3 Father Christmas Parade**
Santa's get-together on the Strøget (page 75)

**4 Copenhagen Jazz Festival**
Jazz on every corner and for many the main reason for their Copenhagen trip (page 75)

**5 Kulturnatten**
A dose of culture for all Copenhageners – until midnight (page 75)

## PUBLIC HOLIDAYS

### 1 January
*New Year's Day*

### March/April
*Easter.* Maundy Thursday, Good Friday, Easter Sunday and Easter Monday are public holidays. Most shops also remain closed on Easter Saturday.

### 16 April
*The Queen's Birthday.* At noon the Queen makes an appearance on the balcony of the Amalienborg Palace – and the Copenhageners turn out to congratulate her.

### April/May
The fourth Friday after Easter has been celebrated for over three centuries as *Store Bededag* (Day of Prayer), a religious holiday.

### 1 May
*Labour Day,* when the Danes only work until noon.

### May
*Ascension Day*, a religious holiday.

### May/June
*Whit Sunday* and *Whit Monday* are not just public holidays, but also days of public celebration. For the last decade or so, the *Copenhagen Carnival* has taken place at Whitsun.

### 5 June
*Constitution Day* commemorates the birth of the democratic constitution in 1849.

### 24-26 December
The Copenhageners love the busy period leading up to the *Christmas Holidays* and the shops stay open until noon on Christmas Eve.

### 31 December
*Nytarsaften.* The Danes work until noon on New Year's Eve.

## SPECIAL EVENTS & FESTIVALS

### March
Fashion and Design Festival in numerous shops and other venues around the city.

## May

Usually held in the last week of May, the *Wonderful Copenhagen Marathon* attracts long-distance runners from all over the world for this 42-km race through the city, to the rapturous applause of the enthusiastic Copenhageners.

## May/June

★ For the last ten years or so, Copenhagen has celebrated its *Carnival* in the Østerbro District, at *Whitsun* and not, as is customary in other Christian countries, immediately prior to Lent. The Danes have chosen the South American variation, with processions of samba dance groups and fireworks as their role model. A huge children's carnival takes place on the Tuesday after Whit Sunday.

## July

★ Every year at the beginning of July, Copenhagen stages its world-famous *Jazz Festival*, with nine days of concerts (some 450 in total) featuring Danish and international jazz musicians. The day's programme starts in the morning and goes on until late at night, many of the concerts taking place on the street in the old town, in the historic squares and along the canals. And they are all free! The clubs and small cafés in Copenhagen, which have long been jazz strongholds in their own right, are an integral part of the Jazz Festival. In the evenings, the stage is set for a broad range of top-class entertainment, covering all shades of the jazz spectrum.

## August/September

*Summer Ballet Festival in Frederiksberg:* The programme of the annual Ballet Festival in Frederiksberg is of truly international calibre. Performances take place at differing venues, and are always in the open. The Copenhageners like to combine the evening performances with a picnic, but during the spectacular performances themselves the baskets remain firmly closed.

Every two even-numbered years, from the end of August to the second week in September, there is the *Golden Days Festival*, a celebration of Danish art and culture from the "Golden Age" from 1800-1850.

Also a biennial event, the Øresund Festival *Kulturbro* (Bridge of Culture) runs for three months from mid-September to mid-December and highlights all aspects of the visual arts and design in the Øresund region. The festival serves to underline the bridge-building qualities of cultural activity between neighbours.

## October

★ ❂ *Kulturnatten:* As part of the "Night of Culture" which takes place on the second Friday in October, museums, churches, galleries, bookshops, theatres and cinemas remain open until midnight and put on all manner of special activities. Sports clubs, the Boy Scout Movement and other groups stage open-air events for the masses who throng the streets on this occasion. The city is a hive of activity, with special buses ferrying the culture freaks from one venue to the next.

## November/December

Last Saturday before Advent: huge ★ *Father Christmas Parade* on the Strøget. There are *Christmas Markets* in the Tivoli Gardens and at the Nyhavn from the end of November to the end of December.

# Out on
# the town

*Most visitors end up at one of the countless jazz clubs – if they
can drag themselves away from the casino, that is*

**A**s the day draws to a close, the cafés and pubs in the pedestrian zones of the inner city begin to fill up. On the Gammel Torv and in Frederiksberggade in particular, there is a wealth of live music to choose from, disco and top-class jazz being the most prevalent styles on offer. What strikes you about Copenhagen is the lack of fixed rules governing what goes on where: the Tivoli amusement park becomes a concert arena, musicians play live in cafés, discos frequently host stage live performances and the night clubs are often nothing but up-market discos or dance clubs. Given the size of the city, Copenhagen really has a lot to offer. Copenhagen is still considered a relatively safe city, so nothing stands in the way of a leisurely evening wander from one "in" place to another, continuing far into the night. One starting point for such a tour is *Kongens Nytorv* with its busy side streets. The *Gothersgade* is also one of the main

*Night owls see Copenhagen from its best side*

centres of evening entertainment. Try to fit in a visit to the *Baron Boltens Gaard,* a carefully renovated building complex, which can be accessed from the Gothersgade and the Store Kongens Gade – don't miss it.

## CASINO

### Radisson SAS
### Scandinavia Hotel          (105/D5)
★ This is a good, old-fashioned casino, where appropriate dress is essential if you want to get in! You must also remember to take along some form of identification document. Copenhagen's Casino, in the SAS Scandinavia Hotel, offers a wide range of games; besides the usual slot machines, there is also blackjack, punto banco, American roulette and classic French roulette. *Daily 2 pm-4 am; SAS Scandinavia Hotel, Amager Boulevard 70; Tel. 33 11 51 15*

## DISCOS

### BIG                        (97/D3)
★ Jungle and techno disco on two floors with a surprisingly good atmosphere. For those of a

## MARCO POLO SELECTION: ENTERTAINMENT

**1  Casino**
French roulette in jacket and tie (page 77)

**2  BIG**
Techno disco with great atmosphere (page 77)

**3  Fever**
Fantastic surroundings in this disco with the built-in view of the stars (page 78)

**4  Palads**
Candy-coloured, palatial cinema showing films in the original language (page 79)

**5  Imperial Kino**
Biggest cinema in Scandinavia with state-of-the-art technology (page 79)

**6  Copenhagen Jazz House**
Jazz at its best (page 80)

**7  Waterloo**
If it must be striptease, then only here (page 81)

**8  Royal Theatre**
A long tradition of superb ballet - book early! (page 81)

more nostalgic nature, there is a separate bar featuring music of the 1960s. There is also a cocktail bar on the roof terrace. Admission prices are staggered according to the sex of the guests and the amount of time they stay. *Fri-Sat, 11 pm-8 am; Lille Kongensgade 16*

**Fever** (97/D3)
★ Red is the dominant colour in this disco for R&B fans, glazed dance floor and view up to the starry sky through translucent red canopy. Passageway links to "Le Kitch" below. *Fri-Sat, midnight-late; Boltens Gård, Gothersgade 8*

**Le Kitch** (97/D3)
Not as pink and plush as the entrance would have you believe. Disco specialising in dance music of the 1970s and 1980s - nothing more and nothing less. Directly underneath the "Fever" disco (passageway links the two). *Fri-Sat, midnight-late; Boltens Gård, Gothersgade 8*

**Pan Disco** (96/C5)
Gay disco, also popular with women and couples. Black, no-frills interior with its own café and cosy club room. Here you can enjoy yourself in a relaxed atmosphere. The "Pan disco" is the real place for fans of funk. *Mon-Fri, 8 pm-5 am, Sat, 8 pm-6 am, Sun, 8 pm-4 am; Knabrostræde 3*

**Rust** (104/A1)
"In" techno disco with live rock sessions in an old, run-down building in the Nørrebro district, which has been livened up with a few licks of colourful paint. Occasional queues to get in. *Mon, 6 pm-midnight, Tues-Thurs, 6 pm-5 am, Fri-Sat, 6 pm-6 am; Gulbergsgade 8*

**Tordenskjold** (97/E4)
Popular, up-to-the-minute disco in classy surroundings. *Daily 10 pm-5 am; Kongens Nytorv 19*

## CINEMAS

For the purists among you, all films are shown here in their original language with Danish subtitles, a real treat for film freaks. Highlight of the cinema-goer's year is the Film Festival in the autumn.

The largest cinema in the city centre is the candy-coloured ★ ‡ *Palads* on the Axeltorv. You'll find the largest concentration of Copenhagen's cinemas in the area around the Town Hall Square, and their programmes are all right up to date. The newest and brightest star in Copenhagen's cinematic heaven is the ★ *Imperial Kino* in the building of the same name near the S-train station Vesterport (**104/A4**). Its 1,000 seats make it the biggest cinema in Scandinavia with the latest state-of-the-art technology.

## CONCERTS

The booklet *Copenhagen this week* contains detailed information on the city's concert diary, for example, the weekly performances of the Radio Symphony Orchestra which give regular Thursday concerts and the Radio Light Orchestra (weekend entertainment programmes) in the *Radiohusets-Konzertsaal,* the concert hall of the broadcasting centre (*Julius Thomsensgade 1)*. (**103/F2**) In the summer, concert-lovers flock to the concert hall in the *Tivoli Gardens,* which plays host to numerous star-studded occasions, some 150 every year. World-famous stars are often among the crowd pullers. The *Museum Louisiana* in Humlebæk has also made a name for itself as a concert venue.

*Like its rivals, the Palads also shows films in the original language*

## MUSIC BARS

### Base Camp Holmen (105/F3)

⚡ On the island of Holmen, originally reserved for military purposes and now gradually being returned to civilian use, a factory building has been transformed into a music bar, disco, nightclub and "the biggest restaurant in the North", boasting tables for 600 diners and its own children's play area. Don't expect any culinary *tours de force* when you come here! The emphasis is very much on do-it-yourself, as you file along the city's longest self-service counter. It all makes for a canteen-like, but highly original atmosphere. There is also an outdoor barbecue, where you can grill your own steaks, etc. The Camp is a popular destination for all age groups, especially families with young children. *Wed, midday-1 am, Thurs, midday-1 am (depending on the entertainment programme, until 5 am), Fri-Sat, midday-5 am, Sun, 11 am-3 pm; Arsenaløen, Halvtorv bygning 148; Tel. 70 23 23 18*

### Club Climax/Mantra (96/A6)

Club on the premises of the former jazz mecca "Slukefter" on the outskirts of the Tivoli Gardens. In keeping with its past, the club now plays probably the best techno and drum'n'bass in town. *Fri only, midnight-6 am; Bernstorffsgade 3; Tel. 33 11 11 13*

### Copenhagen Jazz House (96/C4)

★ ✪ Famous jazz café featuring performances by Danish and international artists. Disco after midnight (from 0.30 am) *Sun-Wed, 6 pm-midnight, Thurs-Sat, 6 pm-5 am; Niels Hemmingsens Gade 10; Tel. 33 15 26 00*

### Fisken (97/E4)

This music pub, located underneath the restaurant Skipperkroen, has a genuine nautical feel to it. *Live music daily, 11 pm-late; Nyhavn 27; Tel. 33 11 99 06*

### Krasnapolsky (96/B5)

⚡ In spite of its plain interior, this agreeable café with its large bar, long wooden benches and generous proportions offers live acts and great atmosphere. *Mon-Wed, 10 am-2 am, Thurs, 10 am-4 am, Fri-Sat, 10 am-6 am, Sun, 2 pm-midnight; Vestergade 10; Tel. 33 32 88 00*

### La Fontaine (96/C5)

Authentic jazz club on the first floor of a half-timbered house; always packed. *Daily 8 pm-6 am; Kompagniestræde 11; Tel. 33 11 60 98*

### Musikcafeen (96/C5)

⚡ Well-known live venue at the Huset Youth Club (main building, 3rd floor). Mixed bag of musical styles, including jazz. *Daily 9 pm-2 am; Rådhusstræde 13; Tel. 33 32 00 66*

### Salon K (96/C5)

The renovated Rococo salon in the Huset Youth Club (main building, 1st floor) serves as a centre for press conferences and presentations during the daytime. In the evening and at night it is an elegant forum for cultural discussions and readings, poetry recitals, revues, chamber music and jazz concerts. *Wed-Sat, 8 pm-2 am; Rådhusstræde 13; Tel. 33 32 00 66*

### Vega (103/E5)

Both mainstream rock bands and alternative artists and groups tread the boards of the small stage at this music club with the 1950s and

1960s look. *Enghavevej 40; phone for details of opening times: Tel. 33 25 80 12*

## NIGHTCLUBS

### Nasa (97/D3)

Up-market club, where the dominant colour is white. If you look the part - no jeans, please - the bouncers will let you ride up to the club entrance in the glass-sided lift. Having got this far, even tourists are permitted to rub shoulders with club members. *Fri -Sat, midnight-late; Boltens Gård, Gothersgade 8; Tel. 33 93 74 15*

### Nautilus (97/F3)

A little on the conservative side, perhaps, but the nightclub in the Copenhagen Admiral Hotel is cosy and popular with guests of all nationalities. *Mon–Thurs, 10 pm–2 am, Fri-Sat, 10 pm–3 am; Toldbodgade 24; Tel. 33 11 82 82*

### New Fellini Club (96/A6)

The nightclub in the Radisson SAS Royal Hotel boasts a unique atmosphere; brilliant interplay of light and sound. *Mon-Wed, 11 pm–5 am, Thurs-Sat, 9 pm-5 am; Hammerichsgade 1; Tel. 33 93 32 39*

### Skovridderkroen (U/E4)

A trip to the Øresund, a little way outside the city, is well worth it. Café, brasserie, restaurant and nightclub near the aquarium. You have to be at least 23 to savour the refined nightclub atmosphere. *Fri-Sat, 11 pm-5 am; Charlottenlund, Strandvejen 235; Tel. 39 46 07 00*

### Waterloo (104/A4)

★One of the most famous nightclubs in Scandinavia, featuring an excellent striptease show. Intimate

*110,000 lights illuminate the Tivoli Gardens every evening*

atmosphere. *Daily 9 pm-5 am; Gammel Kongevej 7; Tel. 33 22 39 46*

## THEATRE

The language barrier presents an almost insurmountable obstacle for the majority of visitors, and this is most keenly felt at the theatre. Most non-Danish speakers only visit the opera (also in Danish) or a ballet performance at the ★ *Royal Theatre (Kongens Nytorv)*. That's why opera and ballet evenings are often booked-up weeks in advance, despite the fact that ballet features on the programme up to three times a week. The works of Danish choreograph Auguste Bournonville (1805-1879) are especially popular. Summer break during June and July. *Ticket reservations: Mon-Sat, 1 pm-7 pm; Tel. 33 69 69 69; ticket sales: Mon-Sat, 1 pm-8 pm; programme information also on the internet at www.kgk-teater.dk*

# Royal landmarks with a hint of Mediterranean flair

*These walking tours are marked in green on the map on the back cover and in the Street Atlas beginning on page 100*

## ① ROYAL COPENHAGEN

**Copenhagen's inner city area is compact and its major sights lie relatively close together. It is therefore possible to explore "Royal Copenhagen" in the course of a two-hour walk. On the way, you will discover evidence of the glorious past of this small kingdom and proof of the modernity of today's monarchy. You might even bump into the Queen, if you're lucky!**

Queen Margrethe II doesn't really mind the competition from Copenhagen's other queen, the Little Mermaid, *Den lille Havfrue (p. 33)*. She lives not far away from the royal residence Amalienborg Palace, at the start of the Langelinie promenade, right next to the marina. The little statue is the subject of more photographs than the Royal Life Guards as they perform the Changing of the Guard ceremony. Japanese guests are wont to roll up their trouser legs and wade out to the famous bathing beauty, just to have their photograph taken with her. Fol-

lowing their audience with the mermaid, only few tourists, though, find their way to the *Citadel (p. 17)*, which is just a stone's throw away. This small town within a town is not at all military, seeming rather to be the light-hearted product of a box of children's building bricks. The tiny museum, dedicated to the Royal Rifle Corps which is housed in the Citadel, has something of a doll's house about it. In stark contrast, the huge *Gefion Fountain (p. 17)* stands on the left in the shadow of the Skt. Albans Kirke, outside the Citadel walls. This monument, which captures the origins of Zealand in stone, is the largest in the city and the only one which can be said to be heroic. Another contrast: from the top step surrounding the fountain, you can look down on the two dainty royal pavilions which stand on the quay, crowned with golden, onion-domed towers. It is here that the Queen and her consort receive state visitors who arrive by ship. The royal party can then proceed on foot along the Amaliegade to the *Amalienborg Palace*

(p. 26). The four palace buildings themselves are not in the least bit brash or showy. Try to time your walk so as to reach the Castle Square by noon, in time for the Changing of the Guard (p. 73), when the soldiers wearing their bearskin helmets - a touch more relaxed than their colleagues in London - parade across the square. They have long since become a trademark of Copenhagen.

For those whose feet are starting to ache, there's an opportunity to rest, just a short distance from the Palace in the direction of the Oslo Quay, in the Amaliehaven (p. 27), a small park with artistic overtones! Don't be tempted to stay too long, though, since Christiansborg, the final stop on this tour, closes at 4 pm.

At the opposite end of the Frederiksgade, in line with the equestrian statue of Frederik V (1746-1766) in the centre of the Castle Square, stands the Marmorkirke (p. 21). It was designed by Nikolai Eigtved, who also drew up the plans for the four Amalienborg Palaces. His original plans foresaw a building which was so immense, that the construction costs threatened to plunge the Royal Family into financial ruin. Even the "light" version is a little on the large side, by Copenhagen's standards. The buildings on the square around the church compensate somewhat for this "giant" among the city's churches.

En route along the Bredgade from the Marmorkirke to the Kongens Nytorv you pass Christian X (1912-1947) looking down from his horse on the Skt. Annæ Plads. The Danes still revere Queen Margrethe's grandfather for his firm stance during the occupation of Denmark by German troops in World War II. The bronze statue on the Kongens Nytorv (p. 25) is of Christian V (1670-1699), the first absolute monarch to rule over the kingdom. It's doubtful, though, whether he would be impressed with the appearance of the square today. There is nothing particularly "regal" about it now; even the Charlottenborg Palace (house no. 1) is no longer a royal residence, but is the seat of the Academy of Fine Arts and its exhibition rooms. The most striking buildings on the square are the legendary Hotel "D'Angleterre" (p. 68) and the no less famous department store, Magasin du Nord, which was once also a hotel. The Royal Theatre is still justified in bearing its title. Queen Margrethe II herself has demonstrated her skills here as a costume designer and is acknowledged to be a true friend of the performing arts. If you retrace your steps a little, you can take a break on the terrace of one of the many restaurants along the cosmopolitan Nyhavn (p. 30). Here, among Danes and tourists from all over the world, looking out towards the wooden ships against the background of picturesque house façades, it is easy to lose all track of time and forget about the walk ahead of you.

Continue along Holmens Kanal – which is not a canal, but the road which links the Kongens Nytorv and the Castle Island Christiansborg – until you reach the Holmens Kirke (p. 21). The older residents of Copenhagen still relate with great enthusiasm how Queen Margrethe and her consort Henrik were married here in June

1967. The style of both ceremony and church were very much to the liking of the Royal Family: down-to-earth and self-effacing. Leaving aside the choir screen and massive pulpit - the largest in the city - only the Royal Gateway is really outstanding. Constructed in 1635, it originally graced the cathedral at Roskilde, and was brought here in 1871 and incorporated into the Holmenskirke. When the Queen, in her capacity as Head of the Church in Denmark, attends a service here, she is just a few steps across the Holmens Bro from the Royal Reception Rooms in *Christiansborg Palace (p. 27)*.

From the outside, the multi-purpose building which houses the Parliament (Folketing) and the Finance Ministry appears rather cold and dull. Had it not been for the terrible fire of 1794, the magnificent Baroque Christiansborg Palace would probably still be standing today. As it is, we can still gain an impression of how it must have looked when we look at the west wing or Ridebane, which was mercifully spared the flames. It still houses the Royal Stables today.

If the walk so far hasn't taken up too much of your time, you can visit the stables and the Carriage Museum, the Royal Court Theatre and Theatre Museum, the Arsenal (Tøjhusmuseet) and, last but not least, the ghostly ruins of Absalon's medieval castle and Copenhagen Castle which are located directly underneath Christiansborg Palace. The nicest place to rest from your Royal Walk is on one of the old, white benches in the *Library Garden (p. 15)*, tucked away behind the Palace in the Tøjhusgade.

However cold and unpleasant the weather is in Copenhagen, the pulsating lifeline of the city, the Strøget, is always buzzing with activity. The 1.8-km-long chain of streets, which was pedestrianised decades ago, exudes an almost Mediterranean flair, 24 hours a day. Here, and in the many side streets, it's easy to get carried away window-shopping and just soaking in the atmosphere. Time flies by, and before you know it, three hours or so have passed - not including coffee breaks!

The Strøget has many faces *(p. 31)*. Seen from the Town Hall Square, the Frederiksberggade is no different from any other pedestrian zone. The twin squares Gammeltorv and Nytorv have unexploited potential. The Caritas Fountain on the Old Market is a magnet for young people, a meeting place from where they move on elsewhere. The nicer cafés, for example, the "Krasnapolsky", are to be found in the *Vestergade,* which runs parallel to the Frederiksberggade. Even the New Market lacks atmosphere on the days when there is no market trade. Things start picking up on the next stretch of the Strøget, *Nyg. Vimmelskaftet.* If you fancy trying the best hot chocolate drink in town, then pop into "La Glace" *(p. 49)*, the café on the corner with Skoubogade. It's noticeable how many of your fellow guests are carrying famous-name carrier bags; as you progress along the Strøget, the shopping experience becomes more exciting, the names of the boutiques have a certain ring to them and the window-dressers pull out all the stops to attract custom. Passing the *Hel-*

*ligåndskirke,* where street musicians of every musical persuasion accompany your every step, you reach the most attractive part of the Strøget, the *Amagertorv (p. 23).* At this point, the road widens as if to make room for the numerous cafés – a good opportunity to take a break and watch the world go by. The shops round about are as refined as the carefully restored half-timbered houses they occupy. The elegance even stretches as far as the public lavatories below the Stork Fountain which adorns the square! It's not hard to imagine that this was the setting, in the 16th and 17th centuries, for great banquets and jousting tournaments. Today the Amagertorv draws people to it like a magnet, pouring in from the side streets: tourists and locals of all ages, young people, mothers pushing prams, elegant ladies on a shopping spree.

The *Købmagergade,* which branches off to the left, is one of the most interesting shopping streets in the city. The shops here may not be quite so up-market, but there are a number of specialists among them, for example, J. Chr. Andersen's cheese shop and delicatessen, Czar. You should also take a look at some of the many side streets, to the left and right of the Købmagergade. In the narrow *Kronprinsensgade* you'll find at No. 5 the tea shop A. C. Perch, which was founded in 1835. Here, time appears to have stood still. In the small, dimly-lit shop the walls are hung with pictures of the generations of proprietors who have run it. The tea is still stored in brass containers and the assortment of goods on sale is made complete by a selection of English teapots and ginger biscuits. Directly opposite stands the colourful "Sommersko" café *(p. 51).* You'll notice that some of the shops bear the sign of the Crown and the inscription "Det Kongelige Hofleverandør", for example, the jeweller's Peter Hertz or Erik Bering's flower shop, exclusive suppliers, in their respective branches, to the Royal Court. Another striking feature is the number of two-in-one shops; one in the basement and a different one on the raised ground floor. The Købmagergade leads to the *Kultorvet (p. 26),* actually a rather ugly square, which gets its charm from the crowds of school children and students who gather here. If you feel like a rest from the colourful hustle and bustle on the streets, why not go and climb up the *Rundetårn (p. 19)*? From the top, there is a wonderful panoramic view across the city. Back on the Amagertorv, you could make another detour, especially if you are interested in antiques, back towards the Town Hall, along the *Læderstræde* and *Kompagnistræde.* Here there is also a string of (basement) cafés and restaurants.

*Østergade* is the last section of the Strøget, which ends at the Kongens Nytorv. The retail *crème de la crème* is here, including the big department stores Illum and Magasin du Nord *(p. 62).* Fans of Danish design – clear-cut, uncomplicated, functional and of high quality - will be spoilt for choice. To round off your tour of the Strøget, why not head for the venerable "Hviids Vinstue" *(p. 55)* on the *Kongens Nytorv* for a glass of wine. If you've still not had enough, and wish to discover the lively side of Copenhagen by night, then carry on to the Nyhavn, where the city's nocturnal heart beats.

# Practical information

*Important addresses and useful information
for your visit to Copenhagen*

## AMERICAN & BRITISH ENGLISH

Marco Polo travel guides are written in British English. In North America certain terms and usages deviate from British usage. Some of the more frequently encountered examples are (American given first):

*baggage = luggage; cab = taxi; car rental = car hire; drugstore = chemist; fall = autumn; first floor = ground floor; freeway/highway = motorway; gas(oline) = petrol; railroad = railway; restroom = toilet/lavatory; streetcar = tram; subway = underground/tube; toll-free numbers = freephone numbers; trailer = caravan; trunk = boot (of a car); vacation = holiday; wait staff = waiter/waitress; zip code = post code.*

## BANKS & MONEY

Banks are open at the following times: *Mon-Wed and Fri, 9 am or 9.30 am-4 pm or 5 pm, Thurs, 9 am or 9.30 am-6 pm, closed Sat-Sun.* It is advisable to wait until you arrive in Copenhagen before you exchange cash. Some banks, for ex-

*The Town Hall - with its statue
of city founder Absalon - is always a
handy point of reference*

ample at the main railway station, in the Tivoli Gardens, at the Tourist Information Office and at the airport offer currency exchange facilities until 9, 10 or even 11 pm. There are plenty of automatic cash dispensers, where you can take out Danish Krone using your credit card and personal code number at any time of the day or night. Eurocheques are accepted up to the value of 1,500 dkr, not just in banks, but also in shops, restaurants and hotels. Credit cards are a very popular means of payment in Copenhagen. The most widely accepted are Eurocard, Visa and Diners. In accordance with Danish law, surcharges may be imposed on payments by credit card. Some restaurants and shops take advantage of the fact and charge a further two per cent of the sum total.

## BEACHES

Copenhagen can't claim to be a seaside resort, but there are several decent beaches in the vicinity, for example, near Dragør on Amager and in Køge Bay to the south of the city. The finest beaches in Zealand are just an hour's drive away.

## CHILDREN

The Danes take their children everywhere with them. Without making any undue fuss, they are integrated into adult life, which means that they are made welcome everywhere they go and treated with patience and care. Public buildings, banks and ferry companies, among others, often provide attractive and imaginative play areas for children.

Most municipal and state-run museums charge no admission fees for children. Buggies are also available for when those little legs go on strike, in some cases prams must be exchanged for one provided by the museum. Most restaurants have special children's menus and highchairs are available as a matter of course.

## CLOTHING

In general, casual clothes are fine for Copenhagen. In restaurants, visitors in jeans and trainers sit alongside businessmen in fine suits and ties. When packing your suitcase, it's more important, even in high summer, to include a pullover and a jacket against the unpredictable coastal climate and the cool evenings, than a gown or a dinner jacket for a night on the town. Don't forget a waterproof!

## CUSTOMS

Travellers from other EU countries are no longer subject to customs checks. Goods for personal use may be brought into and out of the country without restriction (provided they have not been purchased in duty-free shops at airports, in aeroplanes or on ships, in which case import restrictions still apply). In the case of spirits, though, Danish customs officials are very strict. Despite membership of the EU, individual travellers may only bring 1.5 l of spirits into the country.

## CYCLING

Two thousand bicycles, located at 150 prominent positions around the city, are available for anyone to use, free of charge. As is the case with shopping trolleys, they can be removed from stands, using a 20 dkr coin which you reclaim upon return of the bicycle. The following companies also rent out bicycles: *Københavns Cykelbørs; main railway station; Tel. 33 14 07 17* (**96/A6**); *Gothersgade 157; Tel. 33 11 09 09* (**97/D3**); *Dan Wheel "Rent a Bike"; Colbjørnsensgade 3; Tel. 33 21 22 27* (**104/A4**)

## DISABLED PEOPLE

In Denmark, disabled people are integrated into public life as a matter of course. The Danes, in typically uncomplicated fashion, would not dream of excluding a handicapped person and are also most helpful towards strangers with disabilities. Public buildings, most museums and almost all means of public transport have been conceived with the disabled in mind. Most museums have wheelchairs which can be borrowed by visitors. Information about accommodation and other facilities which are adapted to the needs of the disabled is available at every Tourist Information Office in Copenhagen.

## DRIVING

On the road, as elsewhere, the Danes are an easy-going people. This probably has something to do with the speed restrictions in force here; on highways, 110 km/h (68 mph) and overland, 80 km/h (50 mph). The penalties for exceeding the speed limit are very high, and fines imposed on foreigners are to be paid on the spot. Another point to remember is that it is compulsory to drive in daylight with dipped headlights. The network of filling stations is excellent, each supplying leaded petrol (98 octane, 4-star leaded) and unleaded petrol (*Blyfri*, 92, 95 and 98 octane, premium and super) plus diesel fuel. Credit cards are accepted almost everywhere.

## EMBASSIES

### British Embassy
*Kastelsvej 36-40, DK-2100 Copenhagen Ø; Tel. 35 44 52 00; Fax 35 44 52 93; e-mail: britemb@post6.tele.dk.*

### Embassy of the United States of America
*Dag Hammarskøids Allé 24, DK-2100 Copenhagen Ø; Tel. 35 55 31 44; Fax 35 43 02 23; e-mail: usis@usis.dk*

### Canadian Embassy
*Kr. Bernikowsgade 1, DK-2100 Copenhagen K, DK-1105 Copenhagen; Tel. 33 48 32 00; Fax 33 48 32 21.*

## EMERGENCY

Tel. *112,* free of charge from every telephone box.

## FLIGHTS

Copenhagen's airport Kastrup links the city not only to numerous international destinations, but also offers several domestic flights per day to the airports on Jutland (Billund, Esbjerg, Karup, Skrydstrup, Sønderborg, Thisted, Ålborg and Århus-Tirstrup), to Odense on Fyn and Rønne on Bornholm.

SAS (Scandinavian Airlines), *Hammerichsgade 1-5* (**96/A6***); Tel. 70 10 20 00.*

A train departs every ten minutes from the main railway station (**96/A6**) for the airport, and arrives directly underneath Terminal 3. The journey takes approximately ten minutes. There are also frequent bus services from the airport to the main railway station and to Kongens Nytorv.

## HEALTH

Healthcare in Denmark is of a very high standard. In general, emergency treatment is free for foreign visitors. UK passport holders are entitled, under a reciprocal agreement between the Danish and British governments, to at least partial reimbursement of any costs which they may incur (doctor's, dentist's and chemist's fees must be paid on the spot). Don't forget to apply for the E111 entitlement form before leaving home.

For emergencies call 112. Doctors on call in Copenhagen can be reached under *Tel. 33 93 63 00; Mon-Fri, 8 am-4 pm; at all other times, Tel. 38 88 60 41.* Tourist Information Offices have details of how to contact dentists.

Chemists are open as follows: *Mon-Fri, 9 am-5.30 pm, Sat, 9 am-1 pm.* The *Steno Apothek,* directly opposite the main railway station is open 24 hours a day. (**96/A6**), *Vesterbrogade 6C; Tel. 33 14 82 66*

## INFORMATION

### Danish Tourist Board
In the UK:
*55 Sloane Street, London SW1X 9SY; Tel. 020/7259 59 59; Fax 020/ 7259 59 55; e-mail: dtb.london@dt.dk*
In the USA:
*18th Floor, 655 Third Avenue, New York, NY 10017; Tel. 210/ 885 97 00; Fax 210/885 97 26; e-mail: info@goscandinavia.com.*
In Canada:
*Royal Danish Embassy@T03: Suite 450, 47 Clarence Street, Ottawa, Ontario K1N 9K1; Tel. 613/562 18 11; Fax 613/562 18 12; e-mail: danemb @cyberus.ca*

### Københavns Turist Information (104/B4)
Here you can obtain all kinds of information, plus booklets, etc. It is also possible to book individual tours of the city and to find accommodation. *Jan.–April and mid-Sept.–Dec.: Mon–Fri, 9 am–4.30 pm, Sat, 9 am–1.30 pm; May–mid-Sept.: Mon–Sat, 9 am–8 pm, Sun, 10 am– 8 pm; Bernstorffsgade 1, DK-1577 København K; Tel. 33 11 13 25; Fax 33 93 49 69; internet: www.woco.dk*

Two information brochures are available free of charge:

### Copenhagen This Week
Contrary to what you would expect, this English-language brochure appears only once a month. As well as the current Copenhagen events diary, it contains a wealth of information about the city, which should answer any questions you might have.

### Tourist in Copenhagen and North Zealand
This brochure – also in English – cannot be so warmly recommended as the one above, since it consists to a large extent of advertising and, beside the few tips it does actually contain, it conveys a picture of Copenhagen which captures nothing of the city's real charm.

## LOST PROPERTY

### Københavns Politi (U/D5)
*Mon–Thurs, 9 am–5.30 pm, Fri, 9 am–2 pm, closed Sat–Sun; Slotsherrensvej 113; Tel. 38 74 52 61*

### Rail (102/B6)
*Mon–Fri, 9 am–4 pm, Thurs, until 6 pm, closed Sat–Sun; Lyshøjgårdsvej 80; Tel. 36 44 20 10*

### Bus
*For information, call Tel. 36 45 45 45*

## MEASURES & WEIGHTS

| | |
|---|---|
| 1 cm | 0.39 inches |
| 1 m | 1.09 yards (3.28 feet) |
| 1 km | 0.62 miles |
| 1 m² | 1.20 sq. yards |
| 1 ha | 2.47 acres |
| 1 km² | 0.39 sq. miles |
| 1 g | 0.035 ounces |
| 1 kg | 2.21 pounds |
| 1 British ton | 1016 kg |
| 1 US ton | 907 kg |

*1 litre is equivalent to 0.22 Imperial gallons and 0.26 US gallons*

## PARKING

There are only a handful of multi-storey car parks in the city centre, and here you could pay in excess of 15 dkr per hour to park your car. There are a few parking spaces with parking meters and pay-and-display zones which can only be used in conjunction with a parking disc. The old town, however, is rigidly divided into four zones which are subject to charge; here, you must pay for a ticket at one of the ticket machines. They are never far away, but you have to make sure you have enough small change to feed them! In the red zone, you may leave your vehicle for three hours; in the yellow, green and blue zones, similar restrictions apply. Predictably, the most sought-after parking spaces - in front of museums, public buildings, hotels, etc. - are all in red zones. Tickets are compulsory in all zones at the following times, *Mon-Fri, 8 am-6 pm,* in yellow and blue zones also *Sat-Sun, 8 am-2 pm.*

Penalties for illegal parking are high, and the police will not hesitate to tow a vehicle away if necessary. In the case of foreign visitors, they often turn a blind eye and don't bother to follow up payment of parking tickets - but don't count on it!

## POST & TELEPHONE

*Post Offices are generally open as follows: Mon-Fri, 9 am or 10 am-5 pm or 5.30 pm, Sat, 9.30 am-midday. Some remain closed on Saturdays. Occasionally: Mon-Fri, 9.30 am-5 pm.* The Post Office at Købmagergade 33 has extended opening hours: *Mon-Fri, 9.30 am-6 pm, Sat, 10 am-2 pm.* The Post Office at the main railway station: *Mon- Fri, 8 am-10 pm, Sat, 9 am-4 pm, Sun and public holidays, 10 am-5 pm.* The international dialling code for Denmark is 0045. There are no area codes and all direct-dial numbers are eight-digit. From Copenhagen, the international dialling code for Great Britain is 0044, for Canada and the USA, 001. Alongside coin-operated telephone boxes, (25 Øre, 1 dkr, 5 dkr, 10 dkr, 20 dkr and 1 DM coins), you will find an increasing number of cardphones. Telephone cards can be purchased at DSB counters, Post Offices and kiosks. Warning: don't be tempted to stock up on cards for your next trip, since they have a very short expiry date. Calls are charged at a standard rate, even if no connection is made. It is possible to receive calls in a public telephone box; the number is on the notice board.

Directory inquiries (inland): Tel. 118

## PUBLIC TRANSPORT

The bus and S-train networks in Copenhagen are very well developed. There is a uniform fares system for the entire Copenhagen region, which includes transfer tickets and discount cards, plus a 24-hour-ticket which can be used on both buses and trains. The region is divided into 95 zones, which form the basis of fare calculations. Buses and S-trains run from 5 am (on Sundays from 6 am) until around 0.30 am. Between 0.30 am and 5 am, night buses connect most districts with the Rådhuspladsen, leaving the city centre at 1 am, 1.30 am, 2 am, 2.30 am, 3.30 am and 4.30 am (there are also night bus connections to other larger towns).

Tickets can be purchased at stations or on the buses. Twenty-four-hour tickets and the Copenhagen Card, which entitle you to unlimited travel in the entire HT region (the Metropolitan Transport System which covers Greater Copenhagen, i.e. approximately half of Zealand) are available at stations, at all HT ticket outlets and also at Tourist Information Offices. Discount cards for 2, 3 or 5 zones or the entire network are sold at stations and all HT ticket outlets. Discount cards valid for 2 or 3 zones can also be purchased on the buses. Important: don't forget to stamp your ticket in the card-clipping machine at the station or on the bus at the start of your journey! Several people can travel with one discount card at the same time, provided they cancel the corresponding number of journeys on it. Children under 7 years of age travel free. Children between the ages of 7 and 11 must buy either a children's ticket or a children's discount card. Two children travelling together can also use an adult ticket or an adult discount card. The period of validity is very important; for tickets and discount cards valid for 2 and 3 zones, the time limit is one hour, for 4, 5 and 6 zones, an hour and a half, and for the entire network, two hours. Passengers caught travelling without a valid ticket on buses are fined 400 dkr, on trains 600 dkr. *For information on bus timetables, contact Tel. 36 45 45 45; for trains, contact Tel. 33 14 17 01.*

## TAXIS

You can flag down a taxi anywhere. Taxis which are available display a green "FRI" sign. You can also order a taxi by calling the following number: *Tel. 32 51 51 51 .*

## THEATRE TICKETS

### Arte (98/B5)
*Daily 10 am-4 pm; Hvidkildevej 64; Tel. 38 88 22 22*

### Engstrøm & Sødring (97/D-E2-3)
*Mon-Fri, 9 am-5.30 pm, Sat, 9 am-1 pm; Borgergade 17; Tel. 33 14 32 28*

### Theaterbilletter – 1/2 pris (96/B3)
Half-price theatre tickets are on sale in a fine old kiosk close to the Nørreport station. These are last-minute tickets valid on the day of purchase, including, from 5 pm onwards, tickets for the Royal Theatre. Tickets for concerts and other events are also available. *Mon-Fri, midday-7 pm, Sat, midday–3 pm; Nørre Voldgade/ at the corner of Fiolstræde; Tel. 38 88 22 22; S and regional train: Nørreport; bus: 5, 7E, 14, 16, 31, 42,43, 73E, 184*

## TIPPING

It is often maintained that tips are included in prices, which is not entirely true. In Denmark, as is the case anywhere else, every waiter or waitress, hotel porter or taxi driver is happy to see his or her service rewarded with a tip.

## TOURS

### Bus tours
Companies such as Copenhagen Excursions and Viking Bus offer a wide range of city tours, e.g., a short tour (one and a half hours), a city and harbour tour (two and a half hours) and a "Royal Copenhagen Tour" which includes visits to the Christiansborg and Rosenborg Palaces. Information on the

various tours, departure times and prices is available at Tourist Information Offices and in every hotel.

Another interesting variant is the "hop-on, hop-off" city tour offered by one sightseeing company in their open-top bus. The tours start every half hour and cover several Copenhagen highlights. These are listed and described in a brochure which is available on the bus. You can get out at any of the tour stops and rejoin the tour at a later stage. The trip lasts one hour. *End of April-Oct: 10.30 am-4.30 pm;*

*adults: 100, children: 50 dkr (with the Copenhagen Card, adults: 80, children: 40 dkr); Start: Rådhuspladsen (opposite the offices of the newspaper "Politiken")*

### Canal tours
Several companies offer tours of the canals. There are several to choose from, of varying lengths - with or without a guide - through canal network in the old town, the harbour and across to Christianshavn. Points of departure include Gammel Strand (**96/C5**) and Nyhavn (**97/E4**).

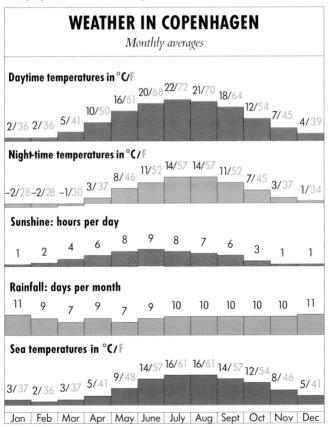

# WEATHER IN COPENHAGEN
*Monthly averages*

**Daytime temperatures in °C/F**

| Jan | Feb | Mar | Apr | May | June | July | Aug | Sept | Oct | Nov | Dec |
|-----|-----|-----|-----|-----|------|------|-----|------|-----|-----|-----|
| 2/36 | 2/36 | 5/41 | 10/50 | 16/61 | 20/68 | 22/72 | 21/70 | 18/64 | 12/54 | 7/45 | 4/39 |

**Night-time temperatures in °C/F**

| -2/28 | -2/28 | -1/30 | 3/37 | 8/46 | 11/52 | 14/57 | 14/57 | 11/52 | 7/45 | 3/37 | 1/34 |

**Sunshine: hours per day**

| 1 | 2 | 4 | 6 | 8 | 9 | 8 | 7 | 6 | 3 | 1 | 1 |

**Rainfall: days per month**

| 11 | 9 | 7 | 9 | 7 | 9 | 10 | 10 | 10 | 10 | 10 | 11 |

**Sea temperatures in °C/F**

| 3/37 | 2/36 | 3/37 | 5/41 | 9/48 | 14/57 | 16/61 | 16/61 | 14/57 | 12/54 | 8/46 | 5/41 |

| Jan | Feb | Mar | Apr | May | June | July | Aug | Sept | Oct | Nov | Dec |

# Do's and don'ts

*How to avoid some of the traps and pitfalls
that may face the unwary traveller*

### Don't despair about the weather

There's not much point getting worked up about the weather in Copenhagen. Being on the coast means it's prone to frequent stiff breezes – and it rains a lot, maybe even for the duration of your holiday. The best thing to do is to take a leaf out of the Copenhageners' book and keep cheerful, even in the midst of a downpour! And don't forget your umbrella!

### Don't photograph Christiania

Fifty thousand visitors per year are burden enough for this urban idyll, but there's one thing which the residents of the "Free City" of Christiania are not prepared to put up with, and that is the sight of hordes of nosy tourists, brandishing cameras and video cameras, on the lookout for the best snapshots.

### Don't take your car

The powers that be in Copenhagen have succeeded in putting drivers off driving! Parking is so heavily restricted and the fines for breaching these restrictions are so high, that it's best just to leave the car on the outskirts of the city and use public transport.

### Don't make fun of the monarchy

The Danes maintain that even opponents of the monarchy are fans of the Royal Family – it sounds like a joke, but there's a grain of truth in it all the same. The monarchy in Denmark is far from being a source of controversy and Queen Margrethe II is extremely popular. This is due, to a large extent, to her stable and unspectacular family circumstances and her surprisingly modest public image – hardly a suitable target for critics and satirists.

### Don't make rash judgements

In Denmark it is perfectly acceptable for people (both men and women) to drink out of a bottle in public – even beer. Someone who chooses to sit down in the sun somewhere with a six-pack at their side, is not automatically an alcoholic, but rather someone who likes to enjoy life.

### Don't get too friendly

The Danes are an extremely friendly and open people, a fact which visitors to Copenhagen will notice immediately. This doesn't mean to say that they are not conscious of a certain distance between themselves and strangers. Therefore it's not advisable to greet everyone you meet with a cheerful *hej*; this is reserved for people who already know each other well. A polite *goddag* will go down a lot better with your hosts.

# Street Atlas of Copenhagen

*Please refer to back cover for an overview
of this Street Atlas*

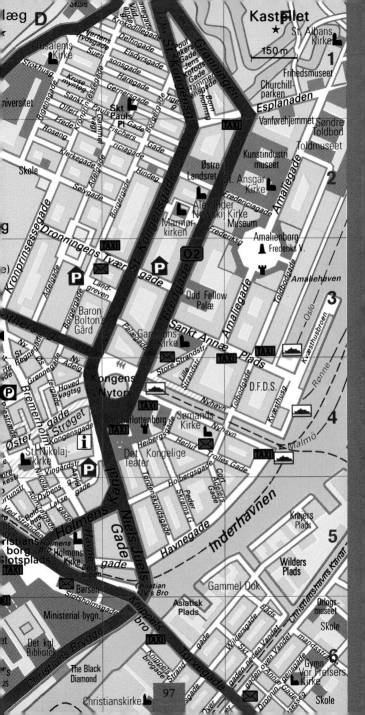

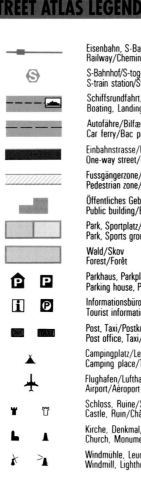

| | | |
|---|---|---|
| ▬▬▬ | | Eisenbahn, S-Bahn/Bane, S-bane<br>Railway/Chemin de fer, Train rapide |
| Ⓢ | | S-Bahnhof/S-tog-station<br>S-train station/Station S |
| | | Schiffsrundfahrt, Anlegestelle/Bådfart, Anlægssted<br>Boating, Landing place/Croisière, Embarcadère |
| | | Autofähre/Bilfærge<br>Car ferry/Bac pour autos |
| | | Einbahnstrasse/Ensrettet trafik<br>One-way street/Rue à sens unique |
| | | Fussgängerzone/Zone for fodgængere<br>Pedestrian zone/Zone pour piétons |
| | | Öffentliches Gebäude/Offentlige bygninger<br>Public building/Bâtiment public |
| | | Park, Sportplatz/Park, Sportsplads<br>Park, Sports ground/Jardin,Terrain de sports |
| | | Wald/Skov<br>Forest/Forêt |
| 🅿 🅿 | | Parkhaus, Parkplatz/Parkeringhus, Parkeringsplads<br>Parking house, Parking place/Parking couvert, Parking |
| ℹ 🅿 | | Informationsbüro, Polizei/Informationskontor, Politi<br>Tourist information center, Police/Syndicat d'initiative, Police |
| ✉ TAXI | | Post, Taxi/Postkontor, Taxi<br>Post office, Taxi/Bureau de poste, Taxi |
| ▲ | | Campingplatz/Lejrplads<br>Camping place/Terrain de camping |
| ✈ | | Flughafen/Lufthavn<br>Airport/Aéroport |
| ♜ ♖ | | Schloss, Ruine/Slot, Ruin<br>Castle, Ruin/Château, Ruine |
| ⬛ ▲ | | Kirche, Denkmal/Kirke, Monument<br>Church, Monument/Eglise, Monument |
| ✗ ➤▲ | | Windmühle, Leuchtturm/Vindmølle, Fyrtårn<br>Windmill, Lighthouse/Moulin à vent, Phare |

| | |
|---|---|
| ▬▬▬ | **Marco Polo Walking Tours** |
| ❶ | Royal Copenhagen |
| ❷ | Lively Copenhagen |

*This index lists a selection of the streets and squares shown in the street atlas*

# INDEX

*This index lists all the main sights and museums, plus important facts and persons mentioned in the guide. Numbers in bold indicate a main entry, italics a photograph.*

# What do you get for your money?

Copenhagen, like Denmark as a whole, is a pricey place for a holiday. In a moderately expensive restaurant, you can expect to pay 25 to 30 dkr for a glass of beer with your evening meal and about 25 dkr for a glass of the house wine. A reasonable bottle of wine will cost you 150 dkr. A glass of the national drink Akvavit costs 30 dkr and a glass of Coca-Cola will set you back 18 dkr. A coffee costs 20 dkr, whereby this means either a whole pot or you can have your cup refilled as often as you like. Cinema fans will have to find around 50 dkr on average for a ticket. Taxi rides are reasonably priced; a journey of five kilometres will set you back approximately 40 dkr. A local telephone call costs 32-34 Øre/minute.

The reserve currency in Denmark is the Krone (abbreviated to dkr or dkk). Banknotes in the following denominations are in circulation: 50, 100, 200, 500 and 1000 dkr, plus the following coins, 25 and 50 Øre, 1 dkr, 2 dkr,

5 dkr, 10 dkr and 20 dkr. One Danish Krone is made up of 100 Øre.

The chart below will give you a rough idea of the exchange rates which your home bank will use for your cheque payments/withdrawals from ATMs.

| DKR | £ | US$ | Can$ |
|---|---|---|---|
| 1 | 0.08 | 0.12 | 0.18 |
| 2 | 0.16 | 0.24 | 0.36 |
| 3 | 0.25 | 0.36 | 0.54 |
| 4 | 0.33 | 0.48 | 0.72 |
| 5 | 0.41 | 0.61 | 0.90 |
| 6 | 0.49 | 0.73 | 1.08 |
| 7 | 0.57 | 0.85 | 1.26 |
| 8 | 0.65 | 0.97 | 1.44 |
| 9 | 0.74 | 1.09 | 1.62 |
| 10 | 0.82 | 1.21 | 1.80 |
| 15 | 1.23 | 1.82 | 2.70 |
| 20 | 1.63 | 2.42 | 3.60 |
| 25 | 2.04 | 3.03 | 4.50 |
| 30 | 2.45 | 3.63 | 5.40 |
| 40 | 3.27 | 4.84 | 7.20 |
| 50 | 4.08 | 6.01 | 9.00 |
| 75 | 6.13 | 9.08 | 13.50 |
| 100 | 8.17 | 12.10 | 18.00 |
| 250 | 20.42 | 30.25 | 44.98 |
| 500 | 40.85 | 60.50 | 89.97 |
| 1000 | 81.69 | 121.01 | 179.93 |